The Hidden Treasure

Lady Umm Kulthum,
Daughter of Imam Ali and Lady Fatima

SUN BEHIND THE CLOUD PUBLICATIONS LTD

In The Name of Allah (swt) the Beneficent, the Eternally Merciful

THE HIDDEN TREASURE

A Sun Behind The Cloud Publication
Published by Sun Behind The Cloud Publications Ltd
Copyright © Jaffer Ladak 2011

ISBN: 978-1-908110-00-8

Cover by Zeenat Datoo
Printed and bound in the United Kingdom by ImprintDigital
Sun Behind The Cloud Publications Ltd
PO Box 15889
Birmingham
B16 6NZ

Learn more about Sun Behind The Cloud Publications Ltd.
Join our mailing list and find out about our latest titles at:

www.sunbehindthecloud.com

I dedicate this book to my beloved mother who inspired me to produce this work, and who always maintains that my Islamic services are due to choosing the topic of Lady Umm Kulthum (s) as my first lecture in Milton Keynes

Jaffer Ladak lives in Milton Keynes, UK, where he is a partner in a firm that supplies medical staff to the NHS and the private sector.

Since returning from a pilgrimage to Makkah (Hajj) in 2005, he was *inspired* to start a systematic study of the Ahlul Bayt (a).

This *journey* has led him to *lecture* in many Islamic centres across Europe, Canada, USA, Dubai, and Kenya; and he regularly appears on AhlulBayt TV.

He has also *guided* *groups* of pilgrims to Saudi Arabia, Syria, Iran and Iraq.

He *studies* courses at the Islamic College in London and private lessons from a student of Ayatollah Syed Kamal Hayderi and Ayatollah Mohammed Sadiq Tehrani.

Jaffer's main areas of interest and study include Qur'anic Commentary, Jurisprudence and History.

Contents

Preface

Over the years I have observed a general trend, that those who are religiously inclined often have an affinity to a particular holy personality.

History provides us with examples of Prophets, noble men and women, saints and martyrs, each with differing dispositions and circumstances. Some have been ridiculed and driven out by their communities, imprisoned or made to live in abject poverty; some have stood tall against the tyrants of their time; others have freed thousands of people.

Each example is a gift from Allah (swt) to teach us how to make righteous decisions and react to situations. More importantly, these examples illustrate that no matter what trial or condition one experiences, there has already been a person who successfully endeavoured through that situation, for the sake of Allah (swt).

Take the story of Prophet Ayyub (a); he was extremely pious and prosperous in what he owned. The arch-deceiver Iblees suggested to Allah (swt) that the reason for his devout worship was due to the blessings he enjoyed. In testing Prophet Ayyub (a) Allah (swt) decided to take away these blessings, including his family, wealth and even health. The Holy Qur'an describes Prophet Ayyub's (a) reaction to these tests when he calls out to his Lord *"Adversity has afflicted me! But You are the Most Merciful of those who show mercy"* (21:83). Despite all the difficulties Prophet Ayyub (a) faced, he turned toward his Lord and kept his faith. As a reward Allah (swt) says *"We responded to him and removed the distresses he had; We gave him his family and the like thereof – a Mercy from Us and reminder to the worshippers"* (21:84).

The experience of gaining and losing worldly blessings is familiar to all people. Prophet Ayyub (a) taught us to act with patience and persistence in faith through trials and misfortunes. We can gain strength from his example with the knowledge that Allah (swt) responds to those who turn to Him.

It is by understanding a holy personality's circumstances that one finds a connection; a source of inspiration to whom they can turn for spiritual support and someone they can aspire to emulate. This connection is by no means restricted to identifying with them through the trials they overcame; sometimes we read a narration, hear a piece of advice or go on pilgrimage to a personality's shrine and this first sparks the relationship. It was through the latter that my mother developed such an affinity to Lady Umm Kulthum (s) and soon after, she introduced her holy personality to me.

Having entered the mausoleum at the entrance of the *Baab Saghir* cemetery in Damascus, my mother and the rest of her group visiting Syria as pilgrims gathered around a shrine. It was said to contain the blessed body of Lady Umm Kulthum (s) or at least be dedicated to her. The group leader, Haji Mohammed Ramzanali (may Allah (swt) grant him a long life to continue serving the Ahlul Bayt (a)) proceeded to recount her life; however, he explained that little information was available about her to the extent that the dates of her birth and death remain disputed and her final resting place is not known for certain. Haji Mohammed concluded his speech with an emotional appeal to the community to research these aspects of her life, to recognise her status and position as the fourth grandchild of the Holy Prophet (s) and the daughter Imam Ali (a) and Lady Fatima (s).

This heartfelt plea had a profound effect on my mother. How could there be so little information about this great personality, she wondered. How could the lovers of the Ahlul Bayt (a) have ignored her role in the history of Islam? The connection was made and the goal became obvious. The plight was not due to her poverty or the message she delivered, but it was in that history had oppressed her and that only through unearthing her legacy and presenting it to the world could we begin to do justice to Lady Umm Kulthum (s). It was through this sorrow and love for Lady Umm Kulthum (s) that my mother asked me to research her unexplored life and in doing so, I was motivated to write this book in the hope that Haji Mohammed's and my mother's devotions are realised. Their devotion became my devotion.

The title of this book, *The Hidden Treasure*, was inspired by the famous statement by Allah (swt) *"I was a hidden treasure; I wanted to be known"*[1]. I felt the saying accurately described her situation in history and more importantly her holy position.

This research has taken almost three years and an abundance of diverse literature and patience. It has been a journey, beginning with importing texts from Beirut, spending time in the Imam Shirazi Library, the libraries at the Al-Mahdi Institute in Birmingham and the Al-Khoei Islamic Centre in London and the bookshops of Damascus. It

1 al-Majlisi, *Bihar al-Anwar*, volume 87, page. 344

has ended with this book and a humble heart which will always be impassioned by Lady Umm Kulthum's (s) cause.

There are two chapters which demanded independent analysis; the chapters on her existence, and her marriage to the second Caliph, Umar al-Khattab. Some of the most eminent Shi'a historians who have written about Lady Umm Kulthum (s) have vehemently disagreed on both these issues and this made it very difficult to draw definite conclusions on these subjects. However, these are not debates that could be ignored, considering the objectives of the book. I felt it was imperative not to begin this study with any preconceived notions that would bias my conclusions. For the analysis of the existence of Lady Umm Kulthum (s), I was assisted by Ayatollah Sheikh Ali al-Hakim of the Islamic College in London who has performed extensive research in this area. The issue of her marriage to Umar required a thorough knowledge of all the views and possibilities. I primarily relied on the book *Zawaaj Umm Kulthum* (The Marriage of Umm Kulthum) by the renowned researcher Sayyid Ali Shahristani[1] to provide me with sources and the perspectives of scholars from both schools of thought; however my conclusions have been predicated on personal observations in addition to those traditionally cited.

This book has been written to inspire all those who love the Ahlul Bayt (a) in the English-speaking world, whether or not they are formally trained in religious sciences. So for the purpose of accessibility, wherever possible, reference has been made to the English version of a book. If the book is available online, the web address has also been cited in the bibliography on page 200. An attempt has also been made to use the vernacular where possible. For example, although in most scholarly works, the followers

---

1 Also the author of *The Prohibition of Recording Hadith*

of the twelve Imams after the Holy Prophet are known as Imami Shi'i Muslims or Shi'ites, here we have referred to them as the Shi'a. All quotes have been referenced using footnotes, where the author, book title, volume and page number have been cited. For those who are interested in researching further, the publication date, publisher and edition can be found in the bibliography.

Throughout the book, effort has been made to refer and commentate on the accounts and narrations attributed to Lady Umm Kulthum (s) from the original Arabic text. This is especially so in the chapter on Lady Umm Kulthum's (s) key contributions in Kerbala, Kufa and Damascus. As with all commentaries, these are based on evidence from the Holy Qur'an, authentic traditions from the Ahlul Bayt (a), an understanding of Islamic Sciences, as well as insighful reflections which have led to an appreciation of what Lady Umm Kulthum (s) may have been alluding to in her speech. Where Arabic words and phrases have been explained, the terms have been transliterated into English and diacritic marks (*harakaat*) have been used to show exact pronounciation. A transliteration table can be found on page 205. I pray that these effort please her.

The Holy Qur'an says "*Surely Allah and His angels bless the Prophet; O you who believe! call for (Divine) blessings on him and salute him with a (becoming) salutation*" (33:56); and He sets an example by sending "*Peace upon His representatives*" (37:181). Following these commands, and with love and respect for great Islamic personalities such as Prophets, Imams, and the purified ladies of the Ahlul Bayt, (a) or (s) has been used after mentioning their names. The (a) for a male individual denotes *Alayhis Salaam* (peace be upon him); the (a) for a group denotes *Alayhim as-Salaam* (peace be upon them); and the (s) for a female individual denotes *Alayhas Salaam* (peace be upon her).

It is my belief that this work is the first dedicated biography or assessment of Lady Umm Kulthum's (s) contributions that exists in any language and therefore, I ardently pray to Allah (swt) that He endorses its content by ensuring it reaches every corner of the world.

I would like to thank all those who participated in bringing this book to fruition: firstly to Sheikh Mohamed 'Abu Jaafar' Saleh for his translations, deep insight and commitment to assisting me and without whom this work would not have been completed. My uncle, Aqeel, for his translations and support; Sister Mariam Kourani for her assitance with checking translation; Sheikh Arif Abdulhussein and Mustafa Field for granting me access to their libraries; the Answering-Ansar team for their research notes; Syed Nadeem Sarwar, Syed Irfan Haider, Abbas and Shabbir Tejani for their moving poetry; those scholars who have read and endorsed the work, especially Sheikh Abbas Jaffer, Brother Yahya Seymour and Syed Mohamed Naqvi, for the time they took to review and critique the book; lastly, Sister Tehseen Merali for her excellent publishing work: your rewards are with Allah (swt).

I pray to Allah (swt) that this pleases Him and the Ahlul Bayt (a) and that in the times of need, Lady Umm Kulthum (s) is there to provide us with her intercession. Ameen.

Jaffer Ladak
Muharram 1433

Introduction

Lady Umm Kulthum (s) was born into the house of Prophethood. She was present during the final period of revelation and witnessed the unravelling of the Muslim *ummah* after the death of her grandfather, Prophet Muhammad (s) and the brutal martyrdom of her mother, Lady Fatima (s). She was the last person to eat with her father, Imam Ali (a) before his head was struck in the mosque of Kufa. She served her brothers Imam Hassan (a) and Imam Hussain (a) especially after the event of Kerbala, whilst heavily chained and imprisoned, being a pillar of strength to her elder sister Lady Zainab (s) and nephew Imam Zain al-Abideen (a).

It is crucial to pause at this juncture and reflect on the statement above, to be conscious of the time in which this lady lived and her direct connection to these holy personalities. This enables the reader to appreciate the extent of her role in the lives of the household of the Prophet (s) and her involvement in the events which have shaped the history of Islam.

Despite her position within the Ahlul Bayt (a) and her contributions to Islamic history, Lady Umm Kulthum (s) has been the forgotten member of the Holy Household. The biographical details of her life are scarce and many scholars have mentioned her only in passing. In fact, many doubt whether she existed at all. Those who doubt her existence have thoroughly researched the information and presented their cases, leaving an imprint on future scholars who then decide whether or not to research her personality further. For those who uphold her blessed existence, she has normally been mentioned by name under the children or siblings of the Infallibles. At best, singular traditions concerning her participation have been mentioned in various books. To my knowledge, history provides no single book dedicated to analysing what is known about her life.

This has left a significant impact on how the Muslim community have understood Lady Umm Kulthum (s); it is as if we have accepted these shortcomings as valid and justifiable. This would not be a legitimate excuse in front of Allah (swt) or his Prophet (s). Allah (swt) tells the Prophet (s) *"Say* [Oh Muhammad]: *I do not ask for any reward* [from you for the deeds I have done] *except love for my nearest of kin and whoever earns good, We give him more of good therein; surely Allah is Forgiving, Grateful"* (42:23).

This shows that loving the Ahlul Bayt (a) is not purposeless, rather it is *good* and by loving them, Allah (swt) will increase us in goodness. The Holy Qur'an explains further in the chapter of The Night Journey that "*if you do good, you do good for your own souls*" (17:7). So the reason why the Prophet (s) asks us to love his family becomes clear "*Say: I do not ask you aught in return except that he who will, may take the way to his Lord*" (25:57). So for those who want to reach nearness to Allah (swt), there is a path; it is the path of Lady Fatima (s), her husband and her children, as the prophetic tradition states "*Verily, as for those who love the household of Muhammad, they will be released from reckoning, measurement of their deeds and passing the discriminating bridge. Verily, as for those who die bearing love for the household of Muhammad, they will die as believers and I guarantee paradise for them*"[1].

Furthermore, the Holy Qur'an has emphasised that we must *"give the near of kin their due rights"* (17:26) and so it is important we study their lives, not only because it is their right, but because we can learn so much from them, as the Holy Qur'an states *"Indeed Allah has chosen (the Prophet) Adam, (the Prophet) Nuh, the descendants of Ibrahim and the descendants of Imran above all nations"* (3:33). The Holy Qur'an warns against taking evil doers or mischief makers as our role models *"lest you harm people out of ignorance"* (49:6); nor to *"take as guardians those who take your religion as a joke"* (5:27).

Lady Umm Kulthum (s) is an exemplary role model; she is the daughter of Lady Fatima (s) and played a significant role in the most important events in the history of Islam. To pay attention to three of the grandchildren of the Prophet (s) and overlook the fourth is unjust. How do her great and noble family feel when we acknowledge and celebrate the births of all her relations *except* her? How do they view the analysis of their traditions and contributions but not hers? Indeed how does she feel about our disregard for her, despite all her suffering for our sake?

This was emphatically answered one day by Lady Umm Kulthum (s) herself when she appeared in a dream to Imam al-Khomeini. The great leader narrates that she presented herself in front of him and stated *"You have mentioned my sister but you have not mentioned me"*.

This humble work attempts to address this unfortunate situation. There have been several works regarding the ap-

1 al-Majlisi, *Bihar al-Anwar*, vol. 27, page 114; see also at-Tabari, *Bisharat al-Mustapha*, page 36. Quoted in: Ibn Shadhan, *One Hundred Virtues of Ali ibn Abi Talib and His Sons, the Imams*, page 90

parent marriage of Lady Umm Kulthum (s) to the second Caliph, and although the issue will be thoroughly examined here, there are broader aims to this book.

The first is to compile the relevant issues of her life into one book. This is an excellent starting point for debating contentious issues including the majority of her biographical information. It will also provide a chronological sequence of events which will put her contributions into perspective, in particular the role she played alongside her sister Lady Zainab (s), after the day of Ashura.

Secondly, this book aims to provide the reader with sufficient information to go beyond a superficial understanding of her life and gain practical lessons from her actions. In order to achieve this, an analysis of her narrations have been included, such as her sermon on the streets of Kufa and her lamentation at the gates of Medina.

Lastly, the book aims to reflect on what we as individuals and as a community that revers the Ahlul Bayt (a) can do to raise awareness about her and the rewards that are attached to engaging in her remembrance.

The objective of this book is to establish a place in our hearts for a member of the Ahlul Bayt (a) who we may not have previously appreciated. Although the majority of her life was spent in some of the most commonly remembered and recounted periods in history, she provides us with an outlook which is both unique and refreshing.

The Name Umm Kulthum

It is unanimously agreed by all historians (who uphold her existence) that the name given to Lady Umm Kulthum (s) when she was born was Zainab, like her elder sister[1]. The majority of scholars have given her the title Zainab *as-Sughra*[2] (the smaller) whilst some have called her Zainab *al-Wusta*[3] (the middle) as they attribute another Umm Kulthum as a daughter of Imam Ali (a) from another wife.

In Arab culture and tradition, it is not customary for a lady to be named Umm Kulthum, rather it is a title known as '*kunya*' (teknonym) which is often used to identify a mother to her first born child. In Arabic, '*Umm*' means 'mother of', so a lady named Umm Kulthum is 'the mother of Kulthum' where Kulthum is the name of her eldest daughter. However, in Arab culture, being called 'mother of...' or 'father of...' is not restricted to the names of children; the practice has also been used to highlight the characteristics or distinctive features of a person. These characteristics can be both positive and negative. In the case of Abu Lahab, mentioned in the Qur'an (111:1) his

---

1 Khafajee, Abd al-Ameer. *Maqatil al-Ma'sumeen*, page 307

2 Hamadani, Ahmed Rahmani. *Fatima Zahra Bahjatu Qalbi Mustapha*, page 650; see also al-Qummi, Asgher Nazim Zadeh, *Hayaat Amir al-Mo'mineen*, the chapter on his children entitled: '*Awlaaduhu*'

3 Shahroodi, Ali. *Mustadrakaat 'Ilm al-Rijaal al-Hadith*, page 559

title or '*kunya*' is used to highlight negative characteristics. Abu Lahab literally means, 'Father of Flames'; this was due to the inflammation of his cheeks and it was also a prophecy of his ultimate destiny.

The title, Umm Kulthum, has been ascribed many meanings by topologists including: 'mother of everything'; 'mother of the beautiful'; and 'mother of the charming'. The word Kulthum also means the 'silk on top of a flag'[1].

Umm Kulthum was also the name of the sister of Prophet Musa (a) who has a cherished position in the history of Islam for the role she played in protecting Prophet Musa (a). The Pharaoh of Egypt had been warned by his soothsayers that a boy would be born who would destroy his kingdom. In an attempt to save his empire, the Pharaoh ordered the killing of every male baby. In fact, many of the men refused to approach their wives for fear of conceiving a son, only for him to be murdered. Prophet Musa's (a) father, Imraan, told the people *"If you want to give up marital relationships, give them up, but he will surely come into this world"*[2]. After the birth, Allah (swt) inspired Prophet Musa's (a) mother: *"Cast him into the river and do not fear nor grieve; surely We will bring him back to you"* (28:7).

Soon after, Lady Asiya (s) the Pharaoh's wife found Prophet Musa (a) floating on the River Nile. She convinced her husband to adopt the child and began a search for a wet nurse. Many nurses attempted, but Prophet Musa (a) would not suckle. Prophet Musa's (a) mother came to know of this and asked her daughter, Umm Kulthum (s), to investigate the situation; the Holy Qur'an explains *"And she said to his sister 'follow him'. So she watched from a distance while they knew not"* (28:11).

---

1 Zubaydee, Maajid Naasir, *500 Questions Regarding the Women around Syeda Zahra*, page 270
2 al-Majlisi, *Hayat al-Qulub*, vol. 1, page 296

Umm Kulthum (s) approached the palace and explained that she knew of a good woman staying nearby who should be given an opportunity to suckle the child. Lady Asiya (s) summoned Umm Kulthum (s), and inquired about the community that the wet nurse was from. She replied that the lady was *"from the family of the Israelites"*. Lady Asiya (s) told her to hurry away, knowing that the Pharaoh would never allow such a lady to suckle the child; however Lady Asiya's (s) maidservants convinced her to let the wet nurse try. Umm Kulthum (s) ran to her mother and brought her to the palace where Prophet Musa (a) began to suckle: Lady Asiya (s) said *"now he is our son"*[1].

Umm Kulthum (s), the sister of Prophet Musa (a), is considered amongst the foremost women of creation. Lady Khadijah (s) has said: *"When Fatima's birth came near, I sent for the Qurayshi midwives, but they refused to help me due to Muhammad (s). During childbirth, four ladies whose beauty and brilliance were indescribable entered the house. One of them said "I am your mother Eve", the second said "I am Asiya bint Muzahim", the third said "I am Umm Kulthum, the sister of Musa" and the fourth said "I am Maryam and we have come to deliver your child". Lady Khadijah (s) continued: "Fatima was then born. When Fatima fell on the ground, she was in the position of prostration, raising her finger"*[2].

As it is generally agreed that Lady Umm Kulthum (s), the daughter of Imam Ali (a) and Lady Fatima (s) never bore a daughter named Kulthum, it can be concluded that this title was given to her as a description of her noble characteristics and disposition. In fact, it is recorded that this title was given to her by the Holy Prophet (s)[3].

1 Ibid, vol. 1, page 297

2 Ordoni, Abu Muhammed, *Fatima the Gracious*, Chapter 6, pages 44 and 45

3 al-Hafnawi, *Fatima Zahra*, the chapter entitled 'Birth of Her Children', page 41

In the same way as Umm Kulthum (s), the sister of Prophet Musa (a), demonstrated bravery, insight and absolute submission to the divine order of Allah (swt), Lady Umm Kulthum (s) exemplifies these very same attributes herself.

The name Umm Kulthum has been used in reference to the daughter of Lady Khadijah (s). There are differing opinions about whether she was the biological daughter of the Holy Prophet (s), Lady Khadijah's (s) daughter from a previous marriage, or Lady Khadijah's (s) niece. However, scholars agree that whatever her exact relationship, she had close proximity to the Prophet (s). Anas Ibn Malik said that *"he saw Umm Kulthum the daughter of the Messenger of Allah wearing a striped silk mantle"*[1]. Sheikh at-Tusi and Syed Ibn Tawus have recommended that blessings be invoked upon this lady through the supplication: *"Oh Allah, send blessings please upon Umm Kulthum, the daughter of Your Prophet. And curse those who injured Your Prophet through wronging her"*[2].

The books of history are replete with instances of this name and a countless number of ladies have enjoyed the nobility of its title, either by being the mother of a daughter named Kulthum, or by being attributed with these righteous characteristics[3].

---

1 *Sahih al-Bukhari*, chapter 80, hadith number 5504; see also hadith number 5465 in different publications

2 For the full supplication, refer to http://www.duas.org/ramazan/salawaat.htm [Accessed on: 03/01/11]

3 These included Umm Kulthum daughters of Abu Bakr, Umar al-Khattab, Jarwila Khuzaima, Asim Ibn Thabit, Uqba Ibn Abu Mu'ayt, Abdul Malik Ibn Marwan, Abdullah bint Aamir, Abdullah Ibn Yazid Ibn Abdul Malik, al-Fadhl Ibn Abbas Ibn Abdul Muttalib and Zainab bint Ali Ibn Abi Talib. This list of ladies bearing the title 'Umm Kulthum' is by no means exhaustive.

The Debate Regarding Her Existence

Scholars often debate contentious issues in Islamic history: these include the events surrounding the death of Lady Fatima (s); whether Fatima as-Sughra and Umm al-Banin were present in Kerbala; who the young daughter of Imam Hussain (a) known as 'Sakinah' was; and the precise date that the Ahlul Bayt (a) returned to Medina after their imprisonment. Each of these discussions requires a meticulous analysis of the facts to reach a conclusion.

The debate over Lady Umm Kulthum (s) is unique, as scholars do not argue over her presence or absence at particular events, rather the speculation is whether she existed at all. This seems peculiar as there are many sources which state that a lady named Umm Kulthum existed and she was the daughter of Imam Ali (a) and Lady Fatima (s). The contention lies with the question of whether this Umm Kulthum was the sister of Lady Zainab al-Kubra (s) or Lady Zainab al-Kubra (s) *herself*.

This chapter is dedicated to assessing the debate over Lady Umm Kulthum's (s) existence according to the opinions of the Shi'a scholars. The examples from researchers who consider Lady Umm Kulthum (s) and Lady Zainab (s) to be the same person from both historical and polemical backgrounds will be presented first. This brings to light the range of arguments generally put forward. In addition, further inquiries will be made which are not usually mentioned by the scholars. Rather, these are popular and thought provoking questions on the subject. Finally, the arguments of a similar range of scholars who uphold the existence of Lady Umm Kulthum (s) will be analysed.

It is my firm belief that Lady Umm Kulthum (s) did indeed exist as the following argument will demonstrate. This discussion is of paramount importance to the followers of the Ahlul Bayt (a), primarily because we are required to internalise a special love for them individually in our hearts. Moreover, the outcome of this debate affects the way we observe the contributions of the daughters of Imam Ali (a) and Lady Fatima (s).

THOSE WHO QUESTION HER EXISTENCE

There are three prominent historians who believe that Lady Umm Kulthum (s) did not exist and that the one reported to be the daughter of Imam Ali (a) and Lady Fatima (s) is in fact, Lady Zainab (s).

Samahat al-Sheikh Abdul Hamid al-Muhajir, in his work *I'ilamu annee Fatima* ('Know that I am Fatima') argues this point, he says:

"Differences of opinion occur regarding Zainab al-Kubra, the heroine of Kerbala and Zainab as-Sughra, famously known as Umm Kulthum. I want to insist there is only

one Zainab who is 'al-Aqeela' and she is the heroin of Kerbala, known as the 'mother of grief'. Those who propagated that Lady Zahra (s) had a daughter, Zainab as-Sughra, who had the epithet Umm Kulthum, did that to associate her to the second Caliph (Umar al-Khattab).

The evidence for this is that when Imam Ali (a) was martyred, he slept that night in the houses of Imam Hassan (a), then Imam Hussain (a) and on the last night in that of Abdullah Ibn Ja'far at-Tayyar. In this last night, narrations say his daughter Umm Kulthum brought him food, but what is known is that Abdullah was married to Zainab al-Kubra and not Umm Kulthum. Thus there is no existence at all as it is alleged by them.

Those who propagated this assumed doubtful narrations, they also thought that Imam Ali (a) gave Zainab as-Sughra to the second Caliph and that she bore Zayd. When you ask about the narration for his existence and where is the evidence of his existence, they will tell you 'a wall fell down on them and they died from this'. This narration is a fallacy and has no authenticity.

Thus, Imam Ali (a) and Lady Fatima (s) did not have any daughter named Zainab as-Sughra but that it was Zainab al-Kubra who was very famous"[1].

Allama Baqir Shareef Qarashi in his book *Hayaat Fatima az-Zahra* ('The life of Fatima az-Zahra') also argues that Lady Umm Kulthum (s) did not exist. He says:

"Some genealogists say that Umm Kulthum was the daughter of Fatima az-Zahra (s) and that Umar al-Khattab married her and that she bore him two children; one was Aun and the other Mu'een. Both were with their mother in Kufa, but that they all died when a wall fell upon them.

---

1 al-Muhajir, *I'ilamu annee Fatima*, vol. 3, page 2

We have refuted this news by clear proof and said that Fatima had no daughter except Lady Zainab (s). Some other researchers have confirmed this fact as well. I found in some sources that Asmaa bint Umays had born from her husband Abu Bakr a son, who was named Muhammad, the immortal martyr, and also had a daughter called Umm Kulthum who grew up in the house of Imam Ali (a) after he had married her mother Asmaa thus Umm Kulthum, whom Umar had married, was Imam Ali's (a) step daughter.

Anyhow, I think, without any doubt, that Fatima az-Zahra had no daughter called Umm Kulthum"[1].

Allama Qarashi mentions elsewhere that *"Zainab was nicknamed as Umm Kulthum. Some historians say that Umm Kulthum was another daughter of Imam Ali (a) and Lady Fatima (s) but we doubt this saying"*[2].

The son of the eminent scholar, Syed Abd al-Razzaq al-Muqarram also contributed to the debate in the preface of his father's book *Maqtal al-Hussain* ('The Killing of al-Hussain'). He wrote:

"The Kerbala epic contains numerous names of men, women, and children in which there is a great deal of confusion with regard to both the names and the ones to whom they were attached. The author (my father) removed such confusion. For example, do you know that those who refer to Umm Kulthum are actually talking about Zainab, the wise lady?!"[3].

This view originates from the scholar Syed al-Muqarram himself who, often when mentioning the name Umm Kulthum would write *"Umm Kulthum, that is, Lady Zainab"* referring to his belief that are the same person[4].

---

1   Qarashi, B., *The Life of Fatima az-Zahra*, page 147

2   Ibid, page 170

3   al-Muqarram, *Maqtal al-Husain*, chapter entitled 'Preface', point 8

4   Ibid, chapter 62 entitled 'Kufa'

An Analysis of Their Views

These three scholars seem to have substantial evidence to support their views. They base their arguments on the premise that Lady Zainab (s) was also known by the epithet 'Umm Kulthum'. For this reason, they argue that any mention of a lady named 'Umm Kulthum' who was the daughter of Lady Fatima (s), refers to Lady Zainab (s) and not a second daughter. There are many other arguments that could be used to strengthen their stance. In the interests of providing a balanced debate, some of these arguments will now be presented.

Firstly, the major biographers of the Ahlul Sunnah community who have afforded great care in compiling the prophetic biography (known as *Seerah*) have not mentioned the birth of Lady Umm Kulthum (s). These biographies include *Seerat Rasool-Allah* by Muhammed Ibn Ishaq. Although the book is currently unavailable, it was copied in part by Ibn Hisham, who also fails to mention the existence of Lady Umm Kulthum (s). In fact, many other biographers have not recorded her birth date.

This inclination is mirrored in the books written by scholars from the Shi'a school of thought. This might seem unusual, especially because there is a great tradition in Shi'a culture of placing emphasis on the birth dates of great personalities and holding large annual celebratory gatherings.

For example it is narrated that upon the birth of Imam Hassan (a), the Holy Prophet (s) asked Imam Ali (a): *"Have you named this blessed child?"* The Imam (a) replied *"I would not precede you, Oh Messenger of Allah"*. In turn the Holy Prophet (s) responded: *"and I would not precede my Lord"* at which point the Archangel Gabriel descended with the name al-Hassan as designated by Allah (swt)

Himself[1]. When Imam Hussain (a) and Lady Zainab (s) were born a similar series of events is widely recorded. It is also mentioned that after the birth of Lady Zainab (s) the Holy Prophet (s) embraced the baby and began to cry. Lady Fatima (s) asked why he was doing this, he replied *"Oh Fatima! Know that after me and you, misfortunes and great calamities will be poured upon this girl"*[2]. These narrations lead us to question why similar traditions are not recorded about the fourth child of Lady Fatima (s).

Furthermore, Lady Umm Kulthum (s) is not regularly mentioned in the books of *Ilm al-Rijal* (translated as 'the knowledge of men'), which is the study of concise biographical evaluation. This study differs from assessing her general presence in the biographies of her relations as it seeks to determine the accuracy of the *chain* of narration or *hadith*. The science, whilst mentioning the primary elements of biographical data such as birth, presence and death also scrutinises each individual who has reported the narration to determine whether or not they can be trusted as a reliable source of information. As the author of a biography may not have considered this aspect of the analysis, the study of *rijal* is a useful alternative source of information.

In this regard, mention of Lady Umm Kulthum (s) cannot be found in:

i.   *Rijal al-Kashshi* by Sheikh Muhammad Ibn Umar al-Kashshi,
ii. *Rijal Ibn Dawood* by Sheikh Dawood al-Hilli,
iii. *Khulaas-atul al-Aqwaal fee Ma'rifatil rijaal* by Allama al-Hilli,
iv. *Rijal al-Burqi* by Sheikh Ahmed Ibn Muhammad al-Burqi,

1 al-Diyarbakri, Hussain, *Tareekh al-Khamees*, vol. 1, page 470
2 Qarashi, *The Life of Fatima az-Zahra*, page 139

v. *Tahdhib at-Tahdhib* by Ibn Hajar Asqalani
vi. *Mu'jam al-Rijal al-Hadith* by Ayatollah Syed Abul Qasim al-Kho'i

The argument that Lady Umm Kulthum (s) did not exist seems quite convincing from these angles. However, as with any debate, arguments must be scrutinised.

The first claim these scholars make is that Lady Umm Kulthum (s) is in fact Lady Zainab al-Kubra (s). Allama Baqir Qarashi is considered to be one the most diligent researchers of this era and his biographical works run into the tens of thousands of pages. It appears both he and Sheikh Abd al-Hamid al-Muhajir have not listed any incident whereby they have recorded Lady Umm Kulthum (s) and Lady Zainab al-Kubra (s) together.

The same however, cannot be said for Syed al-Muqarram, rather there appear to be contradictions in his compilation of the saga of Kerbala, as he narrates traditions where both Lady Zainab (s) and Lady Umm Kulthum (s) are addressed together as individual people. This contradicts his earlier claim that they are the same person. For example he narrates that Imam Hussain's (a) departure intensely grieved the daughters of Banu Abd al-Muttalib who assembled in a group to mourn. He records that Imam Hussain (a) said: *"I plead to you in the Name of Allah not to reveal this matter in disobedience to Allah and His Messenger"*. They replied *"Who should we save weeping and mourning for, since the day of your departure to us is like the demise of the Messenger of Allah (s), that of Ali, Fatima, al-Hassan, Zainab and Umm Kulthum?! We plead to you, may Allah consider us as your sacrificial ransom from your own demise, Oh the one loved by the righteous from among those who reside in the graves!"*[1].

---

1 al-Muqarram, *Maqtal al-Husain*, chapter 21 entitled 'View of the Hashemites'

Furthermore, in the reference section relating to this incident, Syed al-Muqarram quotes that this narration can be found, with varying lines of poetry, in no less than sixteen different books.

In this regard, dozens of scholars who have compiled the story of Kerbala have mentioned Lady Zainab (s) and Lady Umm Kulthum (s) as being together and conversing with each other. Possibly the most important of them all is the book *Maqtal* of Abu Mikhnaf[1] which is unanimously accepted to be the first compilation of the events surrounding Kerbala in history and based on the accounts of seven eye witnesses[2]. Many other scholars have relied on Abu Mikhnaf's narrations, they include: al-Waqidi (d. 207 AH), at-Tabari (d. 310 AH), Ibn Qutaybah (d. 322 AH), al-Mas'udi (d. 345 AH), al-Mufid (d. 413 AH), al-Shahristani (d. 548 AH), al-Khawarizmi (d. 568 AH), Ibn Athir (d. 630 AH) and al-Jawzi (d. 654 AH). Moreover, scholars such as al-Najjashi and Ayatollah Shaheed Muhammad Baqir Sadr have agreed that Abu Mikhnaf is *"a pre-eminent scholar of Kufa"*[3].

Abu Mikhnaf narrates in his *maqtal,* the story of the death of Imam Hussain (a), that as Imam Hussain's (a) horse returned without its rider, Lady Umm Kulthum (s) recited some very moving poetry and then *"leaned toward her sister Zainab"* and continued reciting an elegy about the devastating effects of the lapse of time upon her family[4].

Also considered to be one of the meritorious books of *maqtal* is the *al-Lahuf* by Syed Ibn Tawus. He narrates that

---

1 His full name was Yahya bin Sa'id bin Mikhnaf (d. 157 AH)

2 at-Tabari, M., *Tareekh at-Tabari*, volume 19 entitled 'The Caliphate of Yazid Ibn Mu'awiya'

3 Mavani, Hamid, Forward to *Abu Mikhnaf's Maqtal al-Husayn,* pages 7-10

4 *Maqtal Abu Mikhnaf,* page 150. Quoted from: Shirazi, Hassan, *Mawsu'atu Kamila (Kalimat as-Sayyida Zainab),*page 49

on the night of Ashura, Imam Hussain (a) was surrounded by his womenfolk wailing over his impending martyrdom. He called out to them saying *"Oh Umm Kulthum! And, Oh Zainab!"*[1].

The narration that Lady Umm Kulthum (s) is most famous for is the poetry she recited upon returning to the city of Medina, after the captives were released from prison. Throughout her recitation she addresses members of her family such as the Holy Prophet (s) and Imam Hassan (a), while toward the end she states *"And they took Zainab out of her covering and they hid our belongings"*[2]. This implies that she was speaking about someone else, otherwise it would have been narrated *"and they took me out of my covering"*.

The mention of Lady Umm Kulthum (s) as an individual is not confined to the books of *maqtal*, rather some of the earliest and greatest compilations make clear mention of her such as: *Kitab al-Kafi* by Sheikh al-Kulayni, *Man La Yahdhurhul Faqih* by Sheikh Sadooq and *Kitab al-Irshad* by Sheikh Mufid. As the first two are considered amongst the four greatest collections in Shi'a history and all three authors lived in the earliest periods of occultation, this leaves a distinct historical impression upon the debate.

Whilst it is not necessary to quote every narration where the two sisters (a) are mentioned together or traditions where they are narrated to be talking to or about one another, it is sufficient to say that the number of books and scholars that quote these occurrences run into the dozens. These include narrations about the burial ceremony of Lady Fatima (a) and the period in captivity after Kerbala. In order to appreciate the value of the numerous traditions that narrate the presence of both sisters, it is useful to remember that as the Muslim nation grew and its lands were

---

1 Ibid page 47

2 al-Majlisi, *Bihar al-Anwar*, vol. 45, pages 197-198

expanded, there was no central point in which the scholars acquired their narrations. Some scholars were based in the Hijaz region while others were scattered around Kufa, Damascus, Cairo, Baghdad, Qum and Samarra. They therefore had no geographical connection and little communication which strengthens the validity of their individually recorded narrations concerning the existence of both sisters.

In my opinion, it therefore becomes unlikely that these scholars were involved in a conspiracy to create an additional character in the household of the Prophet (s) in order to verify their claims concerning her marriage to Umar. A distinction must be made between the two issues as one may be inclined to believe in her existence but not marriage to Umar, as opposed to rejecting her existence on the basis of invalidating the marriage to Umar. Furthermore, these narrations were reported and transmitted during the times of many Imams (a), yet there is no mention of the Imams (a) denying her existence

To conclude this section, the primary belief of these scholars is that the two sisters are in fact one person with two names. However, the earliest historical accounts are united in their presentation of Lady Umm Kulthum (s) and Lady Zainab (s) as sisters. As these continue throughout the periods in history without reason to suggest otherwise, the fact that these books were compiled in vastly differing geographical regions and that they can be found in books spanning *hadith*, jurisprudence and history provides sufficient evidence to uphold the existence of Lady Umm Kulthum (s) as the younger sister of Lady Zainab (s).

THE ARGUMENT IN FAVOUR OF HER EXISTENCE

Of course, there are others who argue that Lady Umm Kulthum (s) did in fact exist and that she was the fourth child of Imam Ali (a) and Lady Fatima (s). They argue that although it is regrettable that the birth date of Lady Umm Kulthum (s) is not widely recorded, this is not sufficient evidence to conclude that her birth did not take place.

It is also imperative to keep in mind the style and methodology of the early biographers. In the first two centuries of *hijrah* a biography was commonly known as *Seerah Maghazi* (which literally means 'Stories of Military Expeditions'). These biographies focused specifically on recording of Prophetic incidents such as battles, miracles and narratives pertaining to the Prophet's (s) life. Therefore, they rarely paid attention to issues outside of this such as the births and relations of his extended family. One explanation for the lack of records relating to her birth is that Lady Umm Kulthum (s) was born during the most crucial period of diplomatic and military development under the Holy Prophet (s). It is plausible to postulate that those who narrated the traditions were with the Holy Prophet (s) on the battlefield or recording meetings with kings and ministers from distant lands, and it is possible that mainstream historians have focused on the wider conquests of Islam and have overlooked the birth of Lady Umm Kulthum (s).

Equally, there have been historians who have recorded the existence of Lady Umm Kulthum (s). Among these is one of the earliest historians and greatest scholars of all generations, Sheikh al-Mufid. He saw such vast divisions, even amongst the Shi'a, that he decided to write the book, *Kitab al-Irshad* (The Book of Guidance), on the salient issues about each Imam (a) such as their birth, death, period of leadership, miracles and other incidents to ensure that there was a concise manuscript for anyone who required to know the Imams (a) appointed by Allah (swt)[1]. Approximately half of the book is dedicated to the life of Imam Ali (a) and under the section 'The Children of the Commander of the Faithful' he names twenty seven of the Imam's (a) children including *"Lady Zainab as-Sughra, who was given the title Umm Kulthum. Her mother was Fatima, the blessed, the leader of the women of the worlds"*[2]. Sheikh al-Mufid therefore postulates that Lady Fatima (s) had two daughters: Lady Zainab al-Kubra (s), and Lady Zainab as-Sughra, who is Lady Umm Kulthum (s).

Other scholars following that era continued to receive reports about both sisters, and scholars of the later generations also wrote about Lady Umm Kulthum (s). For example one scholar has written *"Lady Umm Kulthum accompanied her sister Lady Zainab and her noble family which was distinguished with all kinds of merits and purity. She is also among those who succumbed to the injustices of history. She was engulfed in sorrow and pain which even the strongest man cannot dare to relate"*[3].

Syed Asgher al-Qummi mentions in his book *'The Life of the Commander of the Faithful'* in the chapter about the children of the Imam (a) that they were: *"al-Hassan, al-Hussain, Zainab al-Kubra, Zainab as-Sughra known as Umm Kulthum and the one who was miscarried, whom the Prophet (s) called al-Mohsin"*[4]. Furthermore, Sheikh Ahmed al-Hamadani writes *"Lady Umm Kulthum (s) was with Imam al-Hussain and Imam as-Sajjad in Syria and then*

---

1 al-Mufid, *Kitab al-Irshad*, the chapter entitled 'Introduction', page xxvii

2 Ibid, page 268

3 Shakiri, Hussain, *Al Mustapha wal Itrah*, vol. 4, page 151

4 al-Qummi, Asgher Nazim Zadeh, *Hayaat Amir al-Mo'mineen*

back to Medina. She had a very high status, was knowledge-able and eloquent. Her sermon in the presence of Ibn Ziyad is famous[1]. Allama Mamqani also states that *"Lady Umm Kulthum participated in many of the calamities; she followed her sister Lady Zainab in all qualities and was 'the generous' from the house of revelation"*[2].

Perhaps the finest Shi'a historical researcher of recent generations was Allama Syed Murtdha al-Askari. His view was that Lady Umm Kulthum (s) existed and was the daughter of Imam Ali (a) and Lady Fatima (s), due to the narrations he found in such books as: *Futuh al-A'adham, Maqtal al-Khawarizmi, Mudheer al-Ahzaan, al-Luhuf and al-Manaqib* by Ibn Shahr Ashub[3].

Mention of Lady Umm Kulthum (s) can also be found in some books of *Ilm al-Rijal*. However, she has not been mentioned in all books and there are four possible reasons for this. Firstly, the science of *rijal* was introduced in response to a fear that as time moved on, the trustworthiness of a narrator could be forgotten, resulting in their reliability being unknown. As Lady Umm Kulthum's (s) position in the household of the Prophet (s) and her reputation for trustworthiness was established and never disputed, it might have meant that scholars of *Ilm al-Rijal* who often scrutinise the trustworthiness of an individual saw no need to comment on the viability of her narrations.

In the science of *rijaal* there is a category of people known as "those above authentication" (*tawtheeq*) such as Abul Fadhl al-Abbas (a), Lady Zainab (s) and Malik al-Ashtar (a). The high status of Lady Umm Kulthum (a) as a person above authentication is a possible explanation for

1 Hamadani, Ahmed Rahmani, *Fatima Zahra Bahjatu Qalbi Mustapha*, page 123

2 Mamqani, Abdullah, *Tanqeeh al-Maqaal*, the chapter entitled 'The Women'

3 al-Askari, Murtdha, *Maalim al-Madrasatayn*, vol. 3, pages 145-150

her name not being mentioned in these books. Secondly, these scholars may not have narrated any traditions from Lady Umm Kulthum (s) and so her personality might have been irrelevant to their particular field of reference. Thirdly, if the book of *rijal* is an exposition or compilation of another scholar's work who did not mention her, there would be no reason for later scholars to comment on her. Lastly, the scholar may have required a minimum number of narrations from an individual in order to embark on a full investigation into their character. Whilst there are some narrations from Lady Umm Kulthum (s) they are a limited number.

As for those books of *rijal* that do mention her, they include *Adhbat ul makaal fee dhabti asmaa ar-rijal* by Ayatollah Hassan Zadeh Amuli and *Al-Mustadrakaat Ilm ul-Rijaal al-Hadith* by Allama Ali Namazi as-Shahroodi which say: "*Lady Umm Kulthum was with Imam al-Hussain in Kerbala and Imam Zain al-Abideen in Syria and then returned to Medina. She was very high in station, knowledge and eloquence. Her sermon is the gatherings of Ibn Ziyad are well known. She is amongst the noble and trustworthy*"[1]. Although these two scholars are contemporary and their *rijaali* works do not fall into the category of primary resources, it is still worth distinguishing the scholars who uphold her existence based upon their own research.

In this section the additional arguments raised about Lady Umm Kulthum's (s) lack of inclusion in specific biographical works has been addressed. Whilst the arguments have validity, they are not a sufficient to reject her existence all together. On balance, the number of scholars who have reported and confirmed the existence of Lady Umm Kulthum (s) outnumbers those who doubt her existence. This brings about an appreciation of the validity of nar-

1 Shahroodi, *Mustadrakaat 'Ilm al-Rijaal al-Hadith*, Page 559

rating aspects of her life beyond just her birth as sufficient evidence of her life.

OBJECTIONS RAISED BY SHEIKH AL-MUHAJIR

The three scholars mentioned cite their prime belief that Lady Umm Kulthum (s) and Lady Zainab (s) are the same person, however Sheikh al-Muhajir cites particular reasons for his stance. An analysis of these views will follow.

Sheikh al-Muhajir postulates that in the days before the attack on Imam Ali (a), the Imam spent time with each of his children and had a meal at each of their houses. One of the incidents that Lady Umm Kulthum (s) is most famous for is the meal she provided for her father the night before he was attacked. According to Sheikh al-Muhajir, this meal took place at the house of Abdullah Ibn Ja'far, who was the husband of Lady Zainab (s) and therefore, it could not be Lady Umm Kulthum (s) who was with him.

One can argue that not all historians agree that it was the house of Abdullah Ibn Ja'far, rather the majority of quotations cite that it was the house of Lady Umm Kulthum (s). Her name is specifically mentioned without any other attributed to it. As it is not certain that the house belonged to Abdullah Ibn Ja'far, a historian would be inclined to accept the majority of narrations which say it was the house of Lady Umm Kulthum (s).

Even if it were established that the house belonged to Abdullah Ibn Ja'far, this does not counter the possibility that Lady Umm Kulthum (s) was residing in that house as well. In fact, Lady Umm Kulthum's (s) husband was Aun Ibn Ja'far, who was Abdullah's brother; he died in the Battle of Tustar in 19 AH. It is plausible to consider that Lady Umm Kulthum (s) was living with her sister and brother-in-law as a widow after her husband's martyrdom.

The Sheikh's second point raises questions concerning the authenticity of the reports that Lady Umm Kulthum (s) was married to the second Caliph and that they had a son called Zayd. This is because, according to Sheikh alMuhajir, "*When you ask about the narration for his existence and where is the evidence of his existence, they will tell you 'a wall fell down on them and they died from this'. This narration is a fallacy and has no authenticity*"[1]. This argument cannot be considered as a proof that she did not exist as the question of her marriage to the second Caliph is more doubtful than her existence.

It therefore appears that the Sheikh's argument is based on the possibility that the conversation between Imam Ali (a) and Lady Umm Kulthum (s) the night before he was attacked, took place in the house of Abdullah Ibn Ja'far. For this reason, one may be inclined to set aside his argument in the absence of any further evidence supporting his case.

Another reason why Sheikh al-Muhajir's argument could be considered dubious is that amongst the Shi'a scholars he appears to be quite unique in his opinion that *Kitab al-Kafi* by Sheikh al-Kulayni is entirely authentic and holds this view with some fervour. However, in the chapter discussing her marriage, al-Kulayni believes that Lady Umm Kulthum (s) existed and married Umar al-Khattab (under duress) and his works even extend to include an entire section entitled 'The chapter of Umm Kulthum's marriage'. As Sheikh al-Muhajir takes every narration to be entirely authentic and al-Kulayni upholds her existence, one might question why Sheikh al-Muhajir arrived at the conclusion that she did not exist.

---

1 al-Muhajir, *I'ilamu annee Fatima*, vol. 3, page 2

FURTHER DISCUSSION

One final question to answer on the subject of Lady Umm Kulthum's (s) existence is: why is there such a lack of reported material about her? If she was such a noble personality who played an integral role in the history of Islam, why have scholars not struggled to compile a detailed analysis of her life to date? The question requires an analysis of the historical development, circumstances, culture and leadership of the Shi'a community of which a detailed discussion is beyond the scope of this work.

The first observation is that this lack of available material is not unique to Lady Umm Kulthum (s). Unfortunately, there is a lack of detailed information about the lives of many of the greatest female role models in the history of Islam, these include Lady Khadijah (s) the wife of the Prophet (s), Umm Salama (s) and Lady Zainab (s). Perhaps it cannot be considered surprising that the same situation applies to the life of Lady Umm Kulthum (s).

The second reason for the lack of information available, relates to the political circumstances around her life. The Ahlul Bayt (a) lived in considerably restrained and difficult circumstances after the death of the Prophet (s). The Caliphs and enemies of the Holy Household had politically suppressed them and it would be extremely difficult for them to freely express all that they would have wished, for fear of reprisals. However, the few years that Imam Ali (a) was the elected Caliph opened the doors for the women of the Ahlul Bayt (a) to teach and inspire others. It is for this reason that there is a lack of information available concerning her activities before or after that time the period of her father's Caliphate. Lady Umm Kulthum (s) would certainly have shared her knowledge and experiences with the other women of the family and the wives of the companions, hence we do have a handful of narrations from her in this regard, but circumstances would not have allowed her to teach openly.

Thirdly, the doubt casted over the existence of Lady Umm Kulthum (s) by prominent scholars has impacted the way later scholars and researchers have approached the study of her life. Some have also been hesitant to promote the possibility of her marriage to the second Caliph, Umar al-Khattab. Many Shi'a scholars believe that the marriage took place and so disclosing this delicate and somewhat awkward piece of information to the public might be considered as 'conceding ground' on the issue of Imamate and Caliphate. If this is the case, it would be a great shame, as if Lady Umm Kulthum (s) did in fact marry Umar, this would neither reduce her status nor defile her in any way[1].

Perhaps another explanation is that as her birth and death anniversaries are not commonly recorded on Islamic calendars, they are not frequently observed by communities who annually commemorate these important dates for other members of the Ahlul Bayt (a). After generations of omitting her name from calendars and ceremonies, her remembrance in these communities has dwindled.

Lastly, the reason why so little is known about the life of Lady Umm Kulthum (s) is due to her blessed character itself and in many ways can be considered one of the foremost lessons in spiritual disposition *(akhlaq)* and humility. Lady Umm Kulthum (s) was the younger sister of Lady Zainab al-Kubra (s); being the *younger* sister impacted the way she behaved and interacted on a personal and public level. This was out of respect to her sister as according to Imam Zain al-Abideen (a) *"the right of the one older than you is that you should respect him because of his age. You*

1 For more information; see the chapter of this book entitled 'The Debate Regarding Her Marriage'

should recognise his seniority and should not surpass him nor walk ahead of him"[1]. According to the scholars of etiquette, the terms *"should not surpass"* and *"walk ahead"* are not only meant as literal expressions but should become manifest in a person's actions.

To explain the term 'surpass' one may take the example of a person who came to Imam Hassan (a) in need of financial support. The Imam (a) gave what he could, but due to the man's extreme poverty, he still required a greater sum in order fulfil his need. The Imam (a), having nothing more with him sent the man to his younger brother, Imam Hussain (a) to obtain the additional amount. When Imam Hussain (a) met with the man and learnt that his elder brother had provided initial support, he inquired about the amount Imam Hassan (a) had provided. In response, Imam Hussain (a) gave the man his need, but presented one coin less than his elder brother saying *"out of respect to al-Hassan, I cannot give more than what he has already given"*. This is the true meaning of *"not surpassing"* one's elder in knowledge; to be subordinate out of respect.

In a similar way, to not *"walk ahead"* also means to not supersede elder as they have a degree of authority over the younger. Therefore the younger should be submissive to the (legitimate) desires of the elder. This concept can be found in the Holy Qur'an as Prophet Musa (a) turned to Allah (swt), after his people dispute with him, and said: *"My Lord! I have control over none but myself and my brother"* (5:25). The control Prophet Musa (a) speaks of over his brother, Prophet Haroon (a), is neither disrespectful nor domineering; rather it is his rightful authority over his sibling originating from his respect owed to him.

---

1 Imam Zain al-Abideen, *A Divine Perspective on Rights*, Commentry by Mashayekhi, Ghodratullah, page 423,

These narrations clarify the nature of the relationship between Lady Umm Kulthum (s) and Lady Zainab (s). Lady Umm Kulthum (s) would always be submissive to her elder sister and never be desirous of speaking or acting before Lady Zainab (s). This does not mean that she would never step forward to fulfil her responsibilities before Allah (swt), rather unless it was necessary she would allow her elder sister to precede her.

Conclusion

The debate over Lady Umm Kulthum's (s) existence is unique for the followers of the Ahlul Bayt (a). Whilst history often differs on the intention or action of an individual, it is rare to debate a person's actual existence. The result is also significant as if she did not exist, it raises the question about the traditions attributed to her. It is assumed that they would automatically be attributed to the personality of Lady Zainab (s). If however, she did exist it certifies her contributions in Islamic history and establishes the importance of our responsibilities toward her.

The position of the scholars who consider the sisters as one person is based on the narrations that suggest it was actually Lady Zainab (s) who held the title Umm Kulthum. Several arguments are based on the premises that: there is no clear distinction between the sisters; there are narrations which only mention Lady Zainab (s); and that there is significant ambiguity around biographical details of her birth and death. However, the three scholars whose arguments are presented above do not focus on these factors, rather their arguments are based on reported events *during* the life of Lady Umm Kulthum (s).

As scholars unanimously agree that there is a lack of biographical data detailing Lady Umm Kulthum's (s) birth and death, those who suggest that she existed base their arguments on two main types of narrations. These are the narrations which speak of Lady Umm Kulthum (s) alone, and those which mention Lady Umm Kulthum (s) with Lady Zainab (s). One cannot doubt the ramifications of the events of Lady Fatima's (s) and Imam Ali's(a) martyrdoms; the battle of Kerbala; the captivity of the women and children of the family of Imam Hussein; their journey to Kufa and Damascus and the return to Medina. Amongst the Shi'a, these are some of the most recounted narrations all of which mention her as an individual and with her sister. Furthermore, across the entire Muslim nation that included infallible Imams (a), their closest companions, and eventually hundreds of scholars who undertook the utmost precision in discussing and collecting the narrations of these accounts, none of which came across a reason to doubt Lady Umm Kulthum's (s) existence or mention any doubt about it.

It is my opinion that those who argue that Lady Umm Kulthum (s) was in fact Lady Zainab (s) offer no substantial evidence to guarantee this opinion. In fact, there is no decisive narration or event that offers certitude in this light. In fact, over the original period of narration collection, spanning dozens of regions and several centuries, a significant number of traditions have been recorded which distinguish the different personalities and roles of these two great sisters.

Regrettably, there is a lack of attention given to the significant female role models in Islamic history. This hinders the development of the debate as previous generations had not studied her biography, or investigated the doubts over her existence when they were first raised. Not only could this debate have long been clarified, but those who are proponents of her existence would have offered us a deeper insight into her life.

Ultimately, the lack of information about her existence does not prove that she did not exist. When something is rare and precious, its value increases exponentially. Lady Umm Kulthum (s) is a hidden treasure and details of her life are invaluable jewels in the crown of those who strive to love her and seek her proximity.

Her Birth

The birth date of Lady Umm Kulthum (s) is the foundation for two major controversies surrounding her life. The first aspect is in regard to the year in which she was born: views range from the 6th to the 9th year after *hijrah*[1]. From a historical perspective, this is not uncommon as there are often varying dates recorded for the birth and death of members of the Ahlul Bayt (a). For example, Lady Fatima (s) is narrated to have been born either two or five years after the event of revelation; or even before the announcement of Prophethood when the Qurayshi tribes were building the Holy Ka'ba[2].

The date of Lady Umm Kulthum's (s) birth is of particular importance when analysing the narrations concerning her alleged marriage to Umar al-Khattab in 17 AH. If she was born in 9 AH, she would have been considered too young for marriage and this would impact the decency of Umar's request.

The scarcity of narrations reporting her birth also im-

1 The *hijrah* is when the Prophet (s) migrated from Makkah to Medina to escape persecution. Today, the Islamic year is recorded by the number of years 'after hijrah' commonly abbreviated to AH.

2 Ordoni, Abu Muhammed, *Fatima the Gracious*, chapter 6, page 42-43

pacts this discussion. As mentioned in the chapter about her existence, those who argue that Imam Ali (a) and Lady Fatima (s) had three children, often highlight the vast difference in recorded material describing the celebration ceremonies for Imam Hassan (a), Imam Hussain (a) and Lady Zainab (s) compared to those reported for the birth of Lady Umm Kulthum (s).

However, it is reported that: *"The house of Lady Fatima and Imam Ali received their second daughter and fourth child, just as they received their previous children with happiness and gratitude"*[1]. *"She was raised by her mother (and father) in the house that was full of love and faith"*[2].

The account citing the earliest possible birth date states that: *"She was born after Zainab al-Kubra, just as Zainab was born after al-Hussain"*[3]. Imam Hussain (a) was born in 4 AH[4] and Lady Zainab (s) was born in 5 AH[5]. This implies that Lady Umm Kulthum (s) was born in 6 AH[6]. According to several biographers she was born in 7 AH[7].

It is agreed by most historians (who uphold her existence) that the name given to Lady Umm Kulthum (s) when she was born was Zainab, like her elder sister[8]. She has also been named Ruqayya by some historians, however this view is not supported by others.

1   Shakiri, Hussain, *Al Mustapha wal Itrah*, vol. 4, page 151

2   Rai Shahri, Muhammad, *Al-Imam Ali Ibn Abi Talib fil Kitab wa Sunnah wa Tareekh*, vol. 1, page 126

3   Khafajee, Abd al-Ameer, *Maqatil al-Ma'sumeen*, page 307

4   Qarashi, *The Life of Imam al-Hussain*, page 51

5   Qarashi, *The Life of Fatima Zahra*, page 141

6   This is also agreed by the following: Ibn Abi al-Hadeed, *Sharh Nahj al-Balaghah*, vol. 2, page 475; al-Amini, *A'yaan ash-Shi'a*, vol. 7, page 126; Ibn al-Anba, *Umdat at-Talib*, page 54

7   al-Muhajir, Abd al-Hamid, *I'ilamu annee Fatima*, vol. 3, page 2; see also Hamadani, Ahmed Rahmani, *Fatima Zahra Bahjatu Qalbi Mustapha*, page 650; and Dukhayl, Muhammed Ali, *A'laam an-Nisaa*

8   Khafajee, Abd al-Ameer, *Maqatil al-Ma'sumeen*, page 307

It is narrated that *"Fatima was very much in love with the name Zainab because of her* [step] *sister the daughter of the Prophet and in loving her own daughter* [Zainab]. *So when Allah wished her another daughter before the demise of the Prophet, she named her Zainab also but the Prophet gave her the epithet Umm Kulthum"*[1]. In the chapter about her existence, there are various narrations which detail the similarity between the birth ceremonies of Lady Umm Kulthum's (s) elder siblings. The narration about the birth and naming ceremony of Lady Umm Kulthum (s) detailed in the narration above is significantly dissimilar. For example there is no mention of the descent of the Archangel Gabriel from the heavens; nor a mention of the Holy Prophet (s) and his role in naming the child. From this perspective, one may be inclined to reject the narration. However, there are a number of explanations regarding the circumstances surrounding Lady Umm Kulthum's (s) birth which help to account for these differences.

Firstly, the names of Imam Hassan (a), Imam Hussain (a) and Lady Zainab (s) were unique and had not been given to other members of the household of the Prophet (s). However, as Lady Umm Kulthum (s) is reported to have been named 'Zainab' after her elder sister, there may not have been a need to record a separate naming ceremony.

Secondly, as the method, jurisprudence and etiquette surrounding the birth and naming ceremonies had already been recorded for three of the grandchildren of the Prophet (s), it eliminated the need to record any further births.

The third explanation directly relates to the circumstances at the time of Lady Umm Kulthum's (s) birth. It is likely that at this time, the Holy Prophet (s) and Imam Ali (a) would have been on military or political expeditions

1 al-Hafnawi, *Fatima Zahra*, the chapter entitled 'Birth of Her Children', page 41

outside the city of Medina, along with many hundreds of the leading Muslim narrators[1]. In this case, it would have been Lady Fatima's (s) responsibility to name her newborn child. However, the narration does not indicate that she made this decision independently, rather she considered the inclination of her family, as the name of the child may have been discussed beforehand. Furthermore, as the Ahlul Bayt (a) are considered to be *"alike and unalike"*[2], the actions and decisions of Lady Fatima (s) echo those of her father. Therefore, if she were to have named Lady Umm Kulthum (s) in his absence it does not detract from the ceremony in any way as it is as if the Prophet (s) was naming her himself.

Lastly, the honour of naming Lady Umm Kulthum (s) may have been specifically granted to Lady Fatima (s) by Allah (swt) with His knowledge that she would be her last surviving child, as her son after Lady Umm Kulthum (s), Mohsin (a) died during the attack on her house after the death of the Prophet (s).

---

1 For further details, see: Subhani, Ja'far, *The Message*

2 For details about this concept, see: as-Sadr, Mohammed Baqir, *Ahl al-Bayt Tanawwu' Ahdaf wa Wahdah Hadaf*

Lady Umm Kulthum During the Life of the Holy Prophet

The Young Narrator

The Holy Prophet Muhammad (s) is undoubtedly the pinnacle of creation. He is *"a mercy to the entire universe"* (21:107) and *"the most excellent of examples"* (33:21). He was sent to mankind with the mission of *"rehearsing to them the signs, purifying them, teaching them the Book and the wisdom"* (62:2). The Prophet's (s) personality was captivating. People were instantly drawn to him and benefitted from his company; amongst those who spent the most time in his holy presence was his family.

Lady Umm Kulthum (s) spent the early years of her life observing the righteous behaviour and characteristics of her grandfather and adopted his demeanour by observation and imitation.

Islam grew from strength to strength and attracted an increasing number of followers. Whist under the care of her noble grandfather, Lady Umm Kulthum (s) witnessed a number of great events in the history of Islam including its expansion to the surrounding empires; the Battle of Khaybar; her mother being gifted the land of Fadak; the conquest of Makkah; the Battles of Hunayn and Tabuk; the event of Mubahila; the revelation of the Qur'anic chapter of Repentance; the deputation of her father to bring Yemen into the fold of Islam; the farewell pilgrimage; and her father's appointment as the *Master of all Believers* at Ghadir Khumm.

Even though Lady Umm Kulthum (s) was only a few years old at this time, she had the capacity to comprehend the significance of these events. She was not passive, despite her young age, and is a key narrator of the following two events from the life of the Holy Prophet (s).

Firstly, it is narrated by the daughter of Imam Musa al-Kadhim (a) Lady Fatima Ma'suma (s) that Fatima the daughter of Imam as-Sadiq (a) said, that Fatima the daughter of Imam al-Baqir (a) said, that Fatima the daughter of Imam as-Sajjad (a) said, that Fatima and Sakinah the daughters of Imam Hussain (a) said that Lady Umm Kulthum (s) said her mother Lady Fatima Zahra (s) had narrated that she heard her father the Holy Prophet (s) say: "*When I went on the heavenly ascension (Me'raj), I entered heaven and there I saw a palace made of white pearls, the door of which was decorated with pearls and rubies and on that door was hanging a curtain. I raised my head toward it and saw written on the door 'There is no God but Allah, Muhammad is his Messenger and Ali is the guardian of the community.' I then looked at the curtain and it read 'Ah! Ah! Who is like the Shi'a of 'Ali?' I entered the palace and in it saw a castle made of red Aqeeq. It had a door of silver decorated with green topaz and on that door was a curtain hanging. I raised my head and saw written on that door 'Muhammad is the Messenger of Allah, Ali is the successor of the chosen'*"[1].

1 al-Majlisi, *Bihar al-Anwar*, vol. 68, pages 76- 77

Secondly, it is narrated by the daughter of Imam Musa al-Kadhim (a) Lady Fatima Ma'suma (s) that Fatima the daughter of Imam as-Sadiq (a) said, that Fatima the daughter of Imam al-Baqir (a) said, that Fatima the daughter of Imam as-Sajjad (a) said, that Fatima and Sakinah the daughters of Imam Hussain (a) said that Lady Umm Kulthum (s) said her mother Lady Fatima Zahra (s) had said: *"Have you forgotten the words of the Prophet of Allah on the day of Ghadir Khumm when he stated 'whomsoever I am the leader of then Ali is also his leader' and his words to Ali 'your relationship to me is like the relationship of Haroon to Musa'"*[1].

Lady Umm Kulthum (s) was still very young when she lost her beloved grandfather. In the days before his death, a number of the companions desired to see him, but his serious condition meant that only members of his family could visit him[2]. The children of Lady Fatima (s) cried profusely for the loss of their loving grandfather[3].

---

1   al-Amini, *Al-Ghadir,* vol. 1, page 197, Quoted in: Jaffer, M., Lady Fatima Masuma (a) of Qum

2   Subhani, Ja'far, *The Message*, page 775, Quoted in: Jaffer, M., Lady Fatima Masuma (a) of Qum

3   Husayn, Ja'far, *Sirat Ameer al-Mo'mineen*, page 339

Lady Umm Kulthum During the Life of Lady Fatima

A Witness to Calamities

The death of the Holy Prophet (s) saw an immediate change in the outward attitude of many people toward the Ahlul Bayt (a).

Since the establishment of Islam, after the migration to Medina, the unwavering determination and loyalty of Imam Ali (a) had not been met with the same enthusiasm from all, nor were all the companions pleased with his victories on the battlefield or his success in spreading the message of Islam. Some became intensely jealous and this was only fuelled by the way the Prophet (s) loved and preferred the Imam (a) over others.

It is narrated by Imam Ali (a): *"I was going somewhere in Medina with the Holy Prophet, we came towards a garden. I said 'Oh Holy Prophet! How beautiful this garden is!' He replied 'Yes, it is very beautiful and in paradise there will be a more beautiful garden for you'. Then we reached towards another garden and again I said 'Oh Holy Prophet!*

How beautiful this garden is!' And again he said 'Yes, it is very beautiful and in paradise there will be a more beautiful garden for you'. We came across seven gardens and I kept on saying how beautiful they were and he kept replying that there was a better garden for me in paradise. When we left the road, he hugged me and then started crying and said 'May my father be sacrificed for him who is the lone martyr'. I asked 'Oh Prophet of Allah! Why are you crying?' He replied 'My community's hearts are filled with jealousy and they will show this jealousy after my death. That will be the enmity because of (the battles of) Badr and Uhud'"[1].

This enmity and jealousy became manifest after the Holy Prophet's (s) death in the attack on the house of Lady Fatima (s); the demand of allegiance from the Ahlul Bayt (a) and their companions to the new political authorities of Islam; and the confiscation of the land of Fadak from Lady Fatima (s). All these events took place in 11 AH[2]. Lady Umm Kulthum (s) had only just suffered the loss of her grandfather when she was thrust into a series of calamities.

For historians who maintain that Lady Umm Kulthum (s) was born in the 6th or 7th year after *hijrah*, she would have been about four or five years old when she witnessed these calamities. In this way, Lady Umm Kulthum (s) can be compared to another young girl, who at a similar age witnessed hardship on the planes of Kerbala: Lady Sakinah (s), the five year old daughter of Imam Hussain (a).

There are numerous traditions which record the spirituality of Lady Sakinah (s) and how much Imam Hussain (a) loved and cherished her. It is narrated that as Imam Hussain (a) was about to leave for the battlefield, Lady Sakinah (s) stood in his path and said: "*Oh Father have you submitted to death? Whom will I rely on?*". The Imam

1   al-Hilali, Ibn Qays, *Kitab-e-Sulaym*, page 40, hadith number 2
2   For details, refer to: Qarashi, B., *The Life of Fatima az-Zahra*

(a) replied "*Oh Sakinah! How can one without a helper not submit to death? But know, Oh Sakinah, that the mercy and the help of Allah will be with you in this world and the Hereafter. Bear life with patience and do not complain about the decree of Allah. This world is a mere journey and the Hereafter is the perpetual abode*". "*Oh Father in that case take me back to Medina*" pleaded Lady Sakinah (s). "*If the sand grouse is left it will rest in its place*" [meaning that the enemies would not spare him] came the reply. She wept at hearing this. The Imam drew her to his chest and dried her tears as he said "*Oh Sakinah, lengthy will be your grief for me after my death. Do not burn my heart with your tears in regret as long as there is life in my body. After I am killed you are the most worthy to come to my body and weep, Oh the best of women*"[1].

The distress and torment felt by Lady Sakinah (s) on the realisation of the impending martyrdom of her father, and later at the sight of his decapitated body further demonstrates how a young child could feel in this situation of extreme loss, her spiritual status, her extreme sorrow and awareness of the distress felt by her family members.

In the same way, Lady Umm Kulthum (s), would have had the same spirituality and awareness at the equivalent age. The attack on the house of Lady Fatima (s) is one of the most devastating incidents in the history of Islam. The enemies of the Ahlul Bayt (a) surrounded the house, attempted to set fire to it and broke down the door which fell on Lady Fatima (s) who was behind it, pregnant with her unborn child Mohsin (a), who subsequently died in her womb[2]. Lady Umm Kulthum (s) would have been present in that house as it was being attacked and she would have witnessed the way her mother was oppressed.

1 Ishtihardi, *Lamentations II*, page 85. Quoted in al-Qummi, Abbas, *Nafas al-Mahmoom,* chapter 25, section 20

2 For the full narration, refer to: al-Qummi, Abbas, *House of Sorrows* pages 97-100, 103-105, 109-110

The degree of grief felt by the children of Lady Fatima (s) is cited in many books of narration. For example, it has been narrated that: *"Imam Hassan and Imam Hussain entered the house immediately after their mother died and asked Asmaa bint Umais 'Where is our mother?'. Lady Asmaa was overcome with grief and was unable to reply; the two young Imams realising the outcome ran towards the room in which their mother was laid and upon seeing her lifeless body Imam Hussain cried "Oh mother! I am your son Hussain, speak to me before my heart breaks and I die!"*[1].

This level of comprehension and grief extended to all the children of the Ahlul Bayt (a). In fact, one narration states that *"Imam Muhammad al-Jawad, who was less than four years old, was brought to his father* [Imam al-Ridha (a)]. *When he was brought in, he struck his palms upon the ground and raised his head towards the heavens and remained engrossed in deep thought for a long time. Seeing this, Imam al-Ridha asked him 'May I be your ransom! What are you thinking about?' Imam al-Jawad (a) replied 'I am engrossed in thought regarding the sufferings that befell my mother Fatima'"*[2].

Lady Umm Kulthum (s) would have been aware of the debate between her blessed mother and the first Caliph, Abu Bakr, over the confiscation of the land of Fadak. Lady Fatima (s) delivered a compelling sermon to the public attacking the Caliph's legitimacy, knowledge and actions, exemplifying her characteristic of patience and expertise of the Qur'an and prophetic tradition. This would no doubt be something Lady Umm Kulthum (s) committed to memory, as she would later demonstrate the same poise and knowledge when she faced the tyrants of her time.

---

1   al-Qummi, Abbas, *House of Sorrows*, pages 212-213
2   Ibid, page 114

The way Lady Umm Kulthum (s) imitated her mother was the subject of discussion when Abdullah Ibn Abbas (a), the famous commentator of the Holy Qur'an was asked about the deeper meaning of the verse *"And (as for) those who believe and whose offspring follow them in faith, We will unite with them their offspring and We will not diminish to them aught of their work; every man is responsible for what he shall have wrought"* (52:21). He is narrated to have replied that *"This is a metaphor about Zainab and her sister Umm Kulthum, for they will follow their mother on the Day of Judgement"*[1].

Lady Fatima (s) presented Imam Ali (a) with her final will. She then pressed Lady Umm Kulthum (s) to her heart and said to Imam Ali (a) *"And when this daughter of mine reaches maturity, the household articles are for her, and may Allah be her support"*[2]. Lady Fatima (s) then offered some words of advice to her daughters; she said *"My will to you is to participate with your father and brothers to defend Islam. Melt yourself to your brother Hussain (a); his turn will come; he will be the person to carry the command of Allah (swt) and you will be participating with him at that time. You have to share with him everything that will befall his path; be prepared to face even captivity on his path! You have to be for your brothers, care for them and be a mother for them"*[3]. What happened next brings tears to the eyes.

Vivid Portrayal

This section is dedicated to a short commentary on the following hadith:

1 Zubaydee, M., *500 Questions Regarding the Women around Syeda Zahra*, page 272

2 Ibid, page 210

3 Ibid, page 276

ارتفعت ايدي زينب وام كلثوم والحسنين، بالابتهال

الى الله لراحة امهم الزهراء

"*Raising their hands, Zainab, Umm Kulthum and Hassanain were seeking the judgement of Allah (swt) in giving relief to their mother Zahra*"[1] .

A Commentary on this Narration

This narration is an intimate description of how the four children of Lady Fatima (s) were praying to Allah (swt) to give peace to their mother during her final hours. They had witnessed the tragedy of the attack on their house and the deterioration of their mother's strength over the subsequent weeks and were now distraught with the realisation of her impending martyrdom.

The words irtafa'at aydī have been translated as "raising their hands" to describe the position of the children beseeching Allah (swt). This action is considered customary in the etiquette of supplication and represents a needy person, such as when a beggar, who may raise his hands in expectation of the generosity of another.

In Arabic, the word aydin (or root yad) is used to describe the hands but can also refer to the arms too. For example in one verse the Holy Qur'an says: "*Blessed is He whose hands are above the kingdom*" (67:1), while in another it says: "*Oh you who believe, when you stand up for prayer, wash your faces and your hands as far the elbows*" (5:6), thus including the arm. This being the case, the Du'a of Kumayl by Imam Ali (a), says: "*And to you my Lord, I have extended my hand*" (wa ilayka yā Rabbī madadtu yadī) meaning that

1 Zubaydee, M., *500 Questions Regarding the Women around Syeda Zahra*, page 276

not only should one raise their hands in supplication, but also extend *their arms* to receive Allah's (swt) generosity.

This detail makes the above account even more vivid. The children of Lady Fatima (s) raised "their arms" to an 'elevated' or 'lofty' place, which in Arabic is *irtafaʻa*. The Holy Qurʼan uses the same word in several places, including the verses: "*We have made some of these apostles to excel others; among them are they to whom Allah spoke and some of them we raised by many degrees*" (2:253); and when describing Prophet Isa (a): "*Allah raised him up to Himself*" (4:158); and when addressing Prophet Muhammad (s): "*Have We not expanded for you your heart? And raised for you your esteem?*" (94:1-4).

It is also interesting that the children are narrated to have been asking for 'relief' (rāḥah) and not any other word for the improvement in their mother's state. Amongst the root words of rāḥah is rīḥ which means 'wind'. The Holy Qurʼan mentions the wind, not only as a destructive force, but also for the potential benefits it brings. For example in the verses: "*Then We made the wind subservient to him, it made his command to run gently wherever he desired*" (38:36) and "*He it is who sends forth the winds bearing good news before His mercy*" (7:57). The essence of their supplication was for their mother to receive mercy, just as the wind moves about swiftly to deliver 'His mercy'.

We can imagine the scene when Imam Hassan (a), Imam Hussain (a), Lady Zainab (s) and Lady Umm Kulthum (s) gathered around the deathbed of their beloved mother. Not only did they raise their hands in supplication to Allah (swt), but they extended their arms outward and stretched them high, probably above their heads, earnestly seeking an answer to their heartfelt plea. The plea was for His mercy and His relief.

AFTER THE DEATH OF HER MOTHER

When Imam Ali (a) was informed of the death of his beloved wife and companion, he fell down unconscious and after regaining his awareness called out in a grieved voice: "*How should I console myself, Oh daughter of Muhammad? I found comfort in you while you were alive, but now where will I find comfort?*"[1].

The people of Medina cried out and the women of Banu Hashim came to the house of Lady Fatima (s) weeping and wailing. Lady Umm Kulthum (s) stepped out of the house with her face and head covered by a veil which stretched to reach the ground. She called out "*Oh Father! Oh Prophet of Allah! Indeed today we have lost you such that there is no meeting after this!*"[2].

Imam Ali (a) said "*I was busy washing the body of Fatima. Then I anointed her with the left over camphor of the Prophet, shrouded her and just before tying the cord of the shroud I called out 'Oh Umm Kulthum! Oh Zainab! Oh Sakinah! Oh Fidha! Oh Hassan and Oh Hussain! Come and behold your mother for the time for separation has approached'*"[3].

The time Lady Umm Kulthum (s) spent with her mother was irreplaceable. Under her wing, Lady Umm Kulthum (s) had learnt the virtues of piety, chastity and bravery. Lady Fatima (s) was preparing her young daughter to have fortitude and courage in the face of the oppression and to be a pillar of strength to Imam Hassan (a) and Imam Hussain (a), just as she had been to the Holy Prophet (s) and Imam Ali (a).

---

1 Zubaydee, M., 500 *Questions Regarding the Women around Syeda Zahra*, page 213

2 This means 'Oh Prophet, today it is as if we have lost you because we have lost Fatima'.

3 Ibid, pages 213-215

Lady Umm Kulthum During the Life of Imam Ali

Upholding Justice

After the martyrdom of her mother, Lady Umm Kulthum (s) spent thirty years under the care and protection of her father Imam Ali (a). The Imam (a) remarried, and although no woman could ever replace her mother, she was surrounded by the love and support of such lofty women as Lady Fidha (s) and Lady Umm al-Banin (s) as well as her elder sister Lady Zainab (s).

Imam Ali (a) is well known for showing kindness and affection toward orphans and children just as the Holy Qur'an says "*Do good to the parents, the near of kin, the orphans and the needy.*" (4:36). The following story demonstrates the kind of father Imam Ali (a) would have been to Lady Umm Kulthum (s):

Whilst performing *Tawaaf* (circumambulation of the Holy Ka'ba) a man saw two maids talking to each other saying "*I swear to the chosen successor, the just judge, the one with pure intentions and the husband of the pleasant Fatima that it was not like this before.* " The narrator says I asked *"to whom are you referring with these descriptions?"* One of them replied *"I swear to Allah that I am talking about the flag of the scholars, the door of judgement, the divider between paradise and hell, the pious one of the nation, the master of creation, the Prophet's brother, his heir and his successor to his nation; I mean my master, the Commander of the Faithful, Ali Ibn Abi Talib."*

He continued to ask: *"What has he done for you to describe him in this way?"* She replied *"My father was one of Ali's followers and he was killed in the Battle of Siffin. One day Ali Ibn Abi Talib came to our house and my brother and I were blind. When he saw us, he sighed and read out a poem:*

'I have never sighed for anything as much as for children,
Their father was killed and he was once responsible for them,
*   In difficult times, at times of travel and at all times'*

Then he held us close to himself and his blessed hand over our eyes and recited something. When he removed his hand our eyesight had returned and now I can see a camel from kilometres away! This is because of Ali's blessing, may Allah's blessings be upon him" [1].

Lady Umm Kulthum (s) had carefully observed her blessed mother's role as the leader of all women and she surveyed the disposition of her father during the reigns of the first three Caliphs. There were times when the Imam (a) resorted to silence and there were times when it was appropriate to speak out against the injustice. After the assassination of Uthman Ibn Affan, the third Caliph, the Muslim nation turned to Imam Ali (a) saying *"No man has given more distinguished service to Islam, nor is anyone closer to Muham-*

---

1   al-Majlisi, *Bihar al-Anwar*, vol. 41, pages 220-221

mad than you. We consider you to be the worthiest of all men to be our leader"[1]. Imam Ali (a) initially refused, but the people persisted, saying *"We appeal to you in the Name of Allah to accept the leadership. Don't you see the state of the Muslim nation? Don't you see new perils rising everywhere in the lands of Islam? Who will check them if not you?"*[2]. On the 18th of Dhul Hijjah 35 AH, Lady Umm Kulthum's (s) father became the Caliph, exactly twenty three years after he had been formally appointed by the Holy Prophet (s) at Ghadir Khumm.

One of the immediate issues facing the Imam (a) was a group of famous companions who were calling for revenge to be exacted against the killers of the previous Caliph, Uthman. After much diplomacy and many attempts to overcome this irrational trend, it became apparent to the Imam (s) that his opponents were not moving from their position, and thus he began to organise his army to combat their insurgency.

A Peculiar Narration

Here, it must be mentioned that history has recorded a very peculiar incident regarding Lady Umm Kulthum (s) before the Battle of Jamal:

"News reached him [Imam Ali (a)] *that they* [the insurgents] *were heading for the city of Basrah. The people of Medina were stunned by the severity of the discord* [between Imam Ali (a) and the dissidents], *so he sent Kumayl al-Nakha'i to get Abdullah Ibn Umar al-Khattab. When Kumayl brought him, Imam Ali said 'Join up with me' to which Ibn Umar replied 'I am simply one man among them. They have taken up this position and I am in it with them. I am not going to go*

---

1 Ibn Atheer, *Tareekh al-Kamil*, vol. 3, page 98
2 Ibid, page 99

my own way; if they come out to fight against you then so will I; if they decide to hold back, so will I!' Imam Ali tried again and responded *'Then give me surety that you won't come out'* to which Ibn Umar replied *'No, I am not giving you surety'".*

The conversation continued and Imam Ali (a) tried to appeal to Ibn Umar by pointing out that he had known him since his youth, saying *"What about my experience of your abrupt nature as a child and as a man?"* Ibn Umar replied *"You will see another reaction from me"* to which Imam Ali (a) concluded *"Let him be! I will be the surety for him."*.

The narration continues that Ibn Umar returned to Medina where they were saying *"We don't know what to do* [about joining Ali]. *We are dubious about this whole matter. We will stay here until light is thrown upon it and it becomes clear."* Ibn Umar then approached Lady Umm Kulthum (s) explaining what he had heard from the men of Medina about their reluctance to join with her father. Ibn Umar said that he was leaving for the minor pilgrimage but maintaining obedience to Imam Ali (a), except with respect to mobilising forces against him. He then stayed with Lady Umm Kulthum (s).

The next morning someone came to Imam Ali (a) and said *"Something far worse for you than Talha and Zubayr and the Mother of the Believers (A'isha the wife of the Prophet) and Mu'awiya put together happened yesterday".* The Imam (a) asked for clarification and was informed *"Ibn Umar has left for Syria".*

So in response, Imam Ali (a) went to the marketplace, called for riding animals, made men mount them and arranged scouts for each road outside the city; Medina was in commotion. When Lady Umm Kulthum (s) heard what her father was doing, she called for her mule and mounted it. She found the Imam (a) in the marketplace dividing the men into groups to search for Ibn Umar. She addressed her father and said *"What is wrong with you? Don't get worked up about this man! The rumours and tales that have reached you are completely contrary to what has happened; I guarantee for him".* Imam Ali (a) was delighted and said to the riders, who were waiting for instructions, *"You can leave. She didn't lie, nor did he. He has my trust"*[1].

A Commentary on this Narration

The narration portrays the conversation between the Imam (a) and Ibn Umar, one of his opponents. Ibn Umar then approached Lady Umm Kulthum (s) and explained that he was leaving Medina for Makkah the following day. Thereafter a person approached the Imam (a) to inform him that Ibn Umar had departed Medina for Syria in order to join the opposition movement. Imam Ali (a) reacts by organising search parties to patrol the routes between Medina and Syria to catch him. During this commotion, Lady Umm Kulthum (s) leaves her house to inform her father of where Ibn Umar had actually said he is going.

It is most unfortunate that such traditions have managed to be recorded about these noble personalities. Therefore the question must be raised: why has this tradition has been given such credence and prominence in Islamic history? Two explanations come to mind:

Firstly, those who purport that Lady Umm Kulthum (s) did in fact marry Umar al-Khattab, the second Caliph, suggest that this narration illustrates the close relationship between Lady Umm Kulthum (s) and Ibn Umar as the

---

1 at-Tabari, *Tareekh at-Tabari*, the chapter entitled 'The Events of the Year 36', pages 34-35; see also, at-Tabari, *Tareekh at-Tabari*, vol. 4, page 446 (in the original version); Ibn Atheer, *Tareekh al-Kamil*, vol. 2, page 312

son of her husband. They also quote a further narration stating the Ibn Umar led Lady Umm Kulthum's (s) funeral ceremony.

Secondly many historians have attempted to defend the actions of A'isha and her group based on the argument that Imam Ali (a) had not made sufficient attempts to apprehend and punish the killers of Uthman. This narration also attempts to show that the Imam (a) was not in control of the events and was haphazard in his leadership, thereby validating the rebellion of A'isha.

Many contradictions and inconsistencies can be found on close examination of this narration.

Firstly, the conversation between the Imam (a) and Ibn Umar contradicts the majority of other accounts regarding Ibn Umar's stance on the Battle of Jamal. Whilst historians are in agreement that Ibn Umar did not pay allegiance to Imam Ali (a), it is widely recorded that both Talha and Zubayr attempted to pressurise him into joining their group, but he refused saying *"It is better for A'isha to sit at home and not in the canopy upon the camel's back and for both of you to remain in Medina would be better than going to Basrah* [for war with Ali]"[1]. If Ibn Umar was not supportive of the war why would he tell Imam Ali (a) that *"if they come out to fight against you, so will I!"*. This is a further example of contradiction in the content of the narration.

Secondly, one might wonder why Ibn Umar decided to inform Lady Umm Kulthum (s) about the attitude of the people of Medina. Surely Ibn Umar would have spoken to Imam Hassan (a) or Imam Hussain (a). What about the governor of the city? What about his companions? What role had Lady Umm Kulthum (s) played in the politics of the *ummah* to warrant confiding his movements to her? Thirdly, there appear to be contradictions within the narra-

1   Ibn Qutaybah, *al-Imamah wa Siyasah*, vol. 1, page 61

tion. For example Ibn Umar is said to tell the Imam (a) *"I am not giving you surety"* while he tells his daughter that he is *"maintaining obedience to Ali"*. It also states that he said he *"was leaving for the minor pilgrimage"* but also *"stayed with her"*. How can Ibn Umar have both stayed and left for the pilgrimage? What is meant by *"[he] stayed with"* Lady Umm Kulthum (s)? Surely purporting such a statement does not befit the daughter of Lady Fatima (s)? Ibn Umar was the son of the second Caliph and was raised in Medina, why was he unable to find a place to stay elsewhere? Why would the daughter of Imam Ali (a) allow someone who would not support her father to stay in her house?

Fourthly, one might ask, who was the person who informed Imam Ali (a) of Ibn Umar's departure to Syria? What credence did he hold with the Imam (a) that would lead him to organise the people of the city into search parties? We do not find other examples in history where Imam (a) is so easily beguiled by a solitary rumour. Why is this person's name not mentioned in the tradition considering it would have been such an important event? This reaction contradicts other sound narrations which state: *"When Imam Ali's (a) attention was drawn to those men who had not given him their pledge of loyalty, he said that loyalty was not something that could be obtained by force. To be meaningful, he said, it had to be voluntary. Later, it was reported to him that the same men were quietly slipping out of Medina. Ali made no attempt to stop them. He said that under his rule, everyone was free to stay in Medina or to leave it and that he himself was not going to force anyone to stay or to leave"*[1].

The informant states that Ibn Umar's departure to join the forces in Syria was *"worse than Talha and Zubayr and A'isha and Mu'awiya put together"*. Why would Ibn Umar's

---

1 Razawy, Ali Asgher, *A Restatement of the history of Islam and Muslims*, page 547

departure be worse than these personalities joining forces? The former all had more important roles in Islamic history than Ibn Umar; his decision to abstain from assisting the Imam (s) would surely be less problematic than four of Islam's most famous personalities uniting against him in war. Furthermore, if in the narration Imam Ali (a) concludes by stating *"I will be the surety for him"* why would the Imam (a) go against his own position and create a frenzy in Medina the very next day?

Lastly, the narration does not conform to the good etiquette Imam Ali (a) would have taught his beloved daughter Lady Umm Kulthum (s). For her to approach her father, and oppose his decisions publicly is not in keeping with our understanding of her or the behaviour of the womenfolk of Ahlul Bayt (a).

An Insightful Narration

Lady Umm Kulthum (s) did however, have a significant role to play at the time of A'isha's rebellion, and whilst her father and brothers were away defending the religion of Allah (swt) with their bodies and swords, she was in Medina defending it with her actions and words just as she had learnt to do from her blessed mother.

An example of a narration relating Lady Umm Kulthum's (s) role at this time will now follow. The original Arabic of the narration is also included in order to appreciate the eloquence of her words. This will also be discussed in the commentary below.

لَمَّا نزل عليّ عليه السلام بذي قار كتبت عائشة إلى حفصة بنت عمر : أما بعد ، فإنّي أخبرك أنّ عليّاً قد نزل ذا قار ، وأقام بها مرعوباً خائفاً لِمَا بلغه من عدّتنا وجماعتنا ، فهو بمنزلة الأشقر إن

تقدَّم عقر ، وإن تأخّر نحر .

فدعت حفصة جواري لها يتغنّين ويضربن بالدفوف ، فأمرهنّ أن

يَقُلْنَ في غنائهن : ما الخبر ما الخبر ، عليّ في السفر ، كالفرس

الأشقر ، إن تقدَّم عقر ، وإن تأخّر نحر ، وجعلت بنات الطلقاء

يدخلن على حفصة ويجتمعن لسماع ذلك الغناء ؛ فبلغ أمَّ كلثوم

بنت عليّ بن أبي طالب عليه السلام فلبست جلابيبها ، ودخلت

عليهنّ في نسوة متنكّرات ، ثمّ أَسَفَرُتَ عن وجهها ، فلمّا عرفتها

حفصة خجلت وَاسْتَرجَعَت . فقالت أمّ كلثوم :

لأئن ظاهرتما عليه منذ اليوم لقد تظاهرتما على أخيه من قبل

فأنزل الله فيكما ما أنزل . فقالت حفصة : كُفِّي رحمك الله ،

وأمرت بالكتاب فمزّق ....

It is narrated that "*When Imam Ali travelled to Dhiqaar* [an area in southern Iraq which Imam Ali (a) had used as a rendezvous point before engaging in the Battle of Jamal], *A'isha wrote to Hafsa, the daughter of Umar saying: 'Now then! I am informing you that Ali has gone to Dhiqaar and has stayed there in fear and having heard that we are preparing our groups and troops, he is scared. He is like the camel* [waiting to be slaughtered]. *Even if he* [waits there and] *comes later he will still be killed'*".

"*When Hafsa received the letter she called her slave girls and told them to sing and beat drums in celebration of the news. She commanded them to recite in their songs 'What is the news? What is the news? Ali is in his journey, like a black horse. If he proceeds he will be slaughtered, if he delays he will also be killed!' The women of Banu Umayyah were entering* [the house] *in groups all gathering to listen to the songs".*

"News of this gathering reached Lady Umm Kulthum, she dressed herself [covered her face] *and approached the women who were celebrating. Upon entering, she removed the veil from her face and at once Hafsa, recognising her, felt embarrassed and in shock took a step back. Then Lady Umm Kulthum said 'You have been causing mischief toward him just as you have caused mischief before toward his brother [the Prophet (s)] and Allah has revealed about you what he has'. Hafsa responded 'Enough! May Allah have mercy upon you'. Hafsa then asked for the letter from A'isha and tore it up"*[1].

It is also narrated that Lady Umm Salama (s) initially arose [to approach the women who were celebrating] but Lady Umm Kulthum (s) said *"I will go on behalf of you"*[2].

COMMENTARY

The narration describes the atmosphere before the Battle of the Camel. As mentioned, when Uthman Ibn Affan was murdered, the nation turned toward Imam Ali (a) to take the reins of leadership (Caliphate) which he eventually accepted. Many prominent personalities urged immediate investigation into the murder of Uthman. They were dissatisfied with Imam Ali's (a) efforts toward this; his dismissal of certain governors from Uthman's period in leadership; and combined with their general prejudice against him, these personalities united and decided on war; this was to be the second civil war in Islam[3].

1 Shirazi,H., *Mawsu'atu Kamila (Kalimat Syeda Zainab)*, page 42. Quoted from: Bahrani, Hashim, *Awalim Sayida Nisaa*, vol. 2, #1013

2 See al-Madani, Dhamir bin Shadqam, *Waqatal Jamal*, page 32 and al-Majlisi, *Bihar al-Anwar*, vol. 32 page 90

3 The first civil war was the Apostate Wars (*Harub al-Ridda*) led by

The letter provides an insight into the relationship between A'isha and Hafsa, both wives of Prophet Muhammad (s), and indicates that they shared the same view toward Imam Ali (a). When drumming up support for the war, it is narrated that A'isha had approached the other wives to join her and participate in the march from the holy city of Makkah to Basrah, to which all the wives except Hafsa had refused. Despite Hafsa's eagerness to join A'isha she was quickly forbidden by her brother Abdullah Ibn Umar[1].

Although Makkah had been the starting point of the rebellion, there were many supporters of Banu Umayyah in Medina. Some of the people of Medina had started to show enmity towards the household of the Prophet (s), so the celebration at the house of Hafsa would not have come as a surprise to the Medinans. Furthermore, the celebration was a public gathering to the extent that news of the affair reached the house of Lady Umm Kulthum (s). This meant that she was able to attend the gathering and put a stop to it. In this way, Lady Umm Kulthum (s) performed one of the sacred principles of Islam: enjoining good and forbidding evil (*amr bil ma'roof wa nahi anil munkar*).

The narration specifically describes that Lady Umm Kulthum (s) wore the full veil (*jilbaab*) before leaving her house. This action is the manifestation of the verse: "*Oh Prophet! Tell your wives and your daughters and the believing women to put on their outer cloaks (when they go forth). This will be better, so that they should be known and not troubled*" (33:59). Wearing the veil also meant that Lady Umm Kulthum (s) was not recognised by others at the gathering until she approached Hafsa, unveiled herself and rebuked her.

Abu Bakr against those who rejected his Caliphate and paying taxes

1 Razwy, Ali Asgher, *A Restatement of History of Islam and Muslims*, page 452

There must have been something in the facial expression of Lady Umm Kulthum (s) to intimidate Hafsa. She would not have been smiling or happy when she lifted her veil, rather Hafsa would have been faced with the anger in her holy face.

When Lady Umm Kulthum (s) begins to speak out against Hafsa, she uses the words of the Holy Qur'an to support her argument. She reminds Hafsa of the verse of the Qur'an that had been revealed about the mischief caused by her and A'isha towards the Prophet (s). She goes on to rebuke her by describing her actions in the eyes of Allah (swt). Hafsa is devastated by this encounter; she is reminded that Allah (swt) and the Ahlul Bayt (a) are fully aware of all disloyalty.

The words Lady Umm Kulthum (s) uses are "you have been doing mischief" (la in ẓāhartumā 'alayhi) which mirrors the Qur'anic verse *"and if you back each other up in mischief against him (the Prophet Muhammad), then indeed Allah is his guardian, as is (the Archangel) Gabriel, the righteous among the believers and furthermore the angels will also back him up!"* (66:4). This verse in Arabic begins with the words 'wa in taẓāharā 'alayhi', this further demonstrates the similarities in wording.

The word 'ẓāhartumā' is derived from 'muẓāharah' which means to protest or demonstrate against somebody or to express or display something toward somebody. We find this same negative implication used in the Holy Qur'an: *"mischief has appeared on the land and the sea because of what the hands of man have done"* (30:41). Here the word ẓahara is used again.

Scholars of Qur'anic commentary are unanimous that the verse quoted by Lady Umm Kulthum (s) as well as other verses have been revealed about A'isha and Hafsa.

The verse in full states: "*If you both turn toward Allah in repentance, then indeed your hearts are already inclined to this; and if you back each other up in mischief against him (the Prophet Muhammad), then indeed Allah is his guardian, as is (the Archangel) Gabriel, the righteous among the believers and furthermore the angels will also back him up!*" (66:4).

This was revealed in response to the discomfort caused by A'isha and Hafsa to the Holy Prophet (s). When the Holy Prophet (s) visited his wife Lady Zainab bint Jahsh (s), she would often make a drink of honey which the Prophet (s) would enjoy. His love for Lady Zainab (s) created jealousy in the hearts of A'isha and Hafsa. They decided that in order to cause a rift between the Prophet (s) and his wife, and stop him from wanting to visit Lady Zainab (s), they would hold their noses and complain of a bad smell, something they knew would trouble the Prophet (s). It is narrated by A'isha herself that "*Allah's apostle used to drink honey at the house of Zainab the daughter of Jahsh and would stay there with her. So Hafsa and I agreed secretly that when he comes to either one of us, we would say to him 'it seems as though you have eaten maghafir [a foul smelling resin] for I smell in you this maghafir.' We did so and he replied 'No, but I was drinking honey at the house of Zainab and I shall never take it again*"[1].

Ubaid Ibn Umar narrates that A'isha said after this event, the verse was revealed "*Oh Prophet! Why do you forbid yourself that which Allah has made lawful to you? You seek to please your wives! Allah is forgiving and merciful. Allah has sanctioned for you the dissolution of your oaths and Allah is your protector and he is the knowing, the wise (66:1-4)*"[2].

Lady Umm Kulthum (s) quoted this verse in particular to remind Hafsa of the trouble she had previously caused to

1 al-Bukhari, Mohammed Ibn Isma'il, Al-Sahih, vol.3, hadith 4582
2 Ibid, hadith number 4922

the Prophet (s). She then equated the mischief she caused to the Prophet (s) to the way she has treated her father, Imam Ali (a) by saying: "*you have been causing mischief toward him [Imam Ali (a)] just as you have caused mischief before toward his brother [The Prophet (s)]*". This statement shows that there had been no change in the attitudes of Hafsa and A'isha.

Lady Umm Kulthum (s) refers to her father as the 'brother of the Prophet (s)' in order to emphasis the intimacy of their relationship and to remind the gathering of the saying of the Prophet (s) to Imam Ali (a): "*Are you not pleased that you hold the same relation to me as the Harun [Aaron] was to Musa [Moses], except there will be no Prophet after me?*"[1]. In this way, Lady Umm Kulthum (s) tried to awaken the people of Medina to the position her father enjoyed with the Prophet (s), that he was no ordinary man.

She defended her father and Imam (a) at a time and place where people were reviling him and rejoicing in the prospect of his death.

This tradition demonstrates the elevated character of Lady Umm Kulthum (s). To enter a house which is celebrating the impending defeat of her own father requires inner strength and bravery. Lady Umm Kulthum (s) provides her followers with the best example of how to control anger and the tongue when faced with ridicule and harassment. She also demonstrates the eloquence of her mother at a time when it was necessary to speak for the cause of Islam by quoting verses from the Holy Qur'an and the traditions of the Ahlul Bayt (a).

---

1   as-Sayuti, J., *The History of the Khaliphs who took the Right Way*, page 184

Martyrdom of Imam Ali

In the month of Rajab 36 AH, the Imam (a) decided to move the capital of the Muslim nation from Medina to Kufa. Upon his arrival in Kufa, the noblemen requested that he should stay at the governor's palace; however he chose a simple house for himself and his family[1]. Lady Umm Kulthum (s) migrated with her father, and for the first time, she left the city of her grandfather.

Just as the successes of Imam Ali (a) during the establishment of Islam had caused one group of people to rebel, the persistence of Imam Ali (a) to pursue justice and uphold the true religion of Allah (swt) led others to hate the Imam (a). These people conspired to murder the Commander of the Faithful, and Ibn Muljim took the responsibility of committing this most heinous crime.

Imam Ali (a) said to his daughter Lady Umm Kulthum (s) *"Oh my little daughter, there is but a little time left for me to be with you."* She asked *"Why is that, father?"* Imam Ali (a) replied *"I have seen the apostle of Allah (swt) in my sleep. He was rubbing the dust from my face and saying 'Oh Ali! Do not be concerned, you have accomplished what you had to do".* Only three days later, he was struck by that blow to the head. Lady Umm Kulthum (s) cried aloud with sorrow. The Imam (a) asked her *"Do not do that my daughter, for I see the apostle of Allah pointing to me with his hand and saying 'Oh Ali! Come to us for what we have is better for you"*[2].

On the 19th night of the month of Ramadhan, Imam Ali (a) went to his daughter Lady Umm Kulthum's (s) house to break his fast. She offered him a very simple meal: two loaves of barely bread, a bowl of milk and some salt.

---

1 Razwy, Ali Asgher, *A Restatement of History of Islam and Muslims*, page 475

2 al-Mufid, *Kitab al-Irshad*, page 9

When Imam Ali (a) saw the food he said *"Following in the footsteps of the Prophet, I have never had more than one type of food on my spread. Oh daughter! There is accountability for the legitimate and retribution for the illegitimate. Do you want your father to stay longer at the station of accountability on the Day of Judgement? Please remove one of the two things from the spread!"* Lady Umm Kulthum (s) took away the bowl of milk and her father ate a few morsels of the bread with the salt. After the meal, he repeatedly looked up at the stars and said *"By Allah! I am not lying nor am I making a wrong statement! This is the night about which the promise has been made to me!"*[1]. The Commander of the Faithful stayed awake during the night. The following morning, he did not go out to the mosque for the night prayer as was his custom. Lady Umm Kulthum (s) asked him *"what has kept you awake?"*. He replied *"I will be killed if I go out in the morning"*. Then Ibn al-Nabbaah came to him and called him to lead the prayer. He walked out a little way and then returned. Lady Umm Kulthum (s) said *"tell Ja'da to pray with the people"*. He answered *"Yes, tell Ja'da to perform the prayer with the people"* but then said *"(Know) there is no escape from the appointed time"*[2].

Soon the time came for Imam Ali (a) to leave the house to lead the prayers. As he left the courtyard of his house to make the short walk across to the entrance of the mosque, some geese began to run in front of him and began to squawk loudly as if attempting to stop the Imam (a) from entering the mosque where his killer was awaiting him. Someone wanted to move them aside but the Imam (a) said *"Leave them be! After a short time the sounds of crying and wailing will start"*. Lady Umm Kulthum (s) asked *"Fa-*

---

1   al-Asqalani, Ibn Hajar, *Al-Sawa'iq al-Muhriqa*, page 134. Quoted in Husayn, J., *Sirat Amir al-Mu'mmineen*, page 707

2   al-Mufid, *Kitab al-Irshad*, page 9

ther! What sort of things are you saying today?". The Imam (a) replied *"My daughter! These birds cannot speak! Take care of feeding them! If you cannot do that, then you must free them so that they can find their food from the earth"*. Lady Umm Kulthum (s) bid farewell to her father with tears in her eyes"[1].

After her father (a) was attacked during morning prayers the people apprehended Ibn Muljim. The men feared Imam Hassan (a) might also be under attack and rushed to gather around him. While they brought Ibn Muljim in shackles for his crime, Lady Umm Kulthum (s) was weeping and approached him and shouted *"Oh enemy of Allah! You have done no harm to my father! May Allah dishonour you!"* Ibn Muljim replied back *"Then for whom do you weep? By Allah, I bought a sword for 1000 dirhams and I spent another 1000 dirhams on poisoning it. If this blow were to have fallen upon all the people of this town, not one of them would have survived it"*[2].

The people carried the Imam (a) home. Outside the house there was loud lamentation and on hearing these sounds Imam Hassan (a) asked the people to disperse. Asbagh Ibn Nubata, one of the most noble companions of the Ahlul Bayt (a) remained and begged Imam Hassan (a) *"Oh son of the Prophet! I would not like to go without seeing the Commander of the Faithful, please allow me to see one glimpse of him!"* and so he was taken inside the house. Upon entering, he saw the Imam (a) had a yellow cloth tied around his head and that his face had turned yellow from loss of blood and weakness. Asbagh could not control himself and started crying. Imam Ali (a) saw this and said *"Oh Asbagh! Do not cry! I am going towards paradise"*.

1 Husayn, Ja'far, *Sirat Ameer al-Mo'mineen*, pages 707-708

2 at-Tabari, *Tareekh at-Tabari*, vol. 17, the chapter entitled 'The First Civil War', page 218

Asbagh replied "I know you will go to heaven! But I cry because I am being separated from you, now who will take care of us? Who will help the orphans and the widows?"[1].

The Imam (a) spent the nights of the 20th and 21st of the month of Ramadhan in great pain from his wound. Lady Umm Kulthum (s) who had broken her fast with her father the night before, was now broken-hearted and helpless. On the 21st of the month of Ramadhan, Imam Ali (a) breathed his last, having spent every moment of his life in absolute servitude to Allah (swt). Lady Umm Kulthum (s), whose father was the protector of the orphans, became an orphan herself.

Poetry mentioning Lady Umm Kulthum

Abul Aswad ad-Du'ali said:

> *"Oh eye, woe to you! Come to our aid;*
> *do you not weep for the Commander of the faithful?*
> *Umm Kulthum weeps over him, with her tears,*
> *she has seen death.*
>
> *Say to the Khawarij wherever they are*
> *– and may the eyes of the envious never find rest -*
> *'it is in the month of fasting you have distressed us,*
> *through the best of all men together!'*
>
> *You have killed the best of those who mounted steeds*
> *and tamed them,*
> *and of those who mounted the ships,*
> *of those who wore sandals*
> *and cut them to measure*

---

1   Husayn, Ja'far, *Sirat Ameer al-Mo'mineen*, page 710

and those who recited the Mathani[1] and the Clear[2]

All the qualities of good were in him
and the love of the Messenger of the Lord of the Worlds

The Quraysh knew, wherever they were,
that you were the best of them in standing and in religion

When I looked toward the face of the father of Hussain,
I saw the full moon over the face of the onlookers
Before his killing we were in good;
we would see the master as said by the
Messenger of Allah amongst us

He was establishing the truth without doubting it
and he was just to his enemies
as he was to his close relatives

He would not conceal any knowledge that he had
and he did not have the character of the haughty ones

It is as if when the people lost Ali,
they were ostriches bewildered in a land for years

Do not rejoice at our affliction
Oh Mu'awiya Ibn Sakhr
for the rest of the successors are from us!"[3]

---

1 This refers to the chapter of The Opening, al-Fatiha, which is chapter 1 of the Holy Qur'an

2 This refers to the 'Clear Book' which is the Holy Qur'an

3 as-Sayuti, J., *The History of the Khaliphs who Took the Right Way*, page 205

The Debate Regarding Lady Umm Kulthum's Marriage to Umar al-Khattab

The controversy of Lady Umm Kulthum's (s) marriage to the second Caliph, Umar al-Kattab is one of the most debated issues in Shi'a Islamic history. From the perspective of the Sunni school of thought, there is no doubt that the marriage took place and united Umar to the Ahlul Bayt (a), however it has divided scholars within the Shi'a sect and has been a cause of disagreement between teachers and their students. In this regard Ayatollah Syed Ali Milani states that "*It has become overwhelming the (amount of) research on the marriage of the Commander of the Faithful Ali's daughter to Umar bin al-Khattab since the early centuries. Many a thesis has been written about it*"[1].

The issue refers to the early years of Umar's Caliphate

---

1 Milani, A., *Khabr Tazweej Umm Kulthum min Umar*, page 6 (can be accessed on www.alhassanain.com in Arabic)

when it is narrated that he approached Imam Ali (a) for the hand of Lady Umm Kulthum (s). His proposal was based on a Prophetic tradition which negates the value of all associations in the hereafter, except those associations with the Holy Prophet (s). Imam Ali (a) is said to have initially rejected the offer, however it is reported that he later agreed and decided to marry the second daughter of Lady Fatima (s) to Umar.

The union between Lady Umm Kulthum (s) and Umar al-Khattab is seen to be unsuitable and strange to some because of the public disapproval of Umar in the Shi'a school of thought. This disapproval is based on a number of incidents including: his rejection of the Treaty of Hudaybiyyah; the incident of 'Black Thursday' when he denied the Prophet (s) a pen and paper to bequeath some final words of advice to the Muslim nation; Umar's central role in usurping Imam Ali (a)'s leadership rights after the death of the Prophet; and his participation in the death of Lady Fatima (s) and her open hatred of him.

The secondary reason why the marriage is contentious pertains to the details of Umar's approach to Imam Ali (a). These details include the maturity of Lady Umm Kulthum (s) and whether she was of marriageable age; the rationale behind and method of the approach to Imam Ali (a) and whether the Imam (a) had been forced to accept; and lastly Umar's behaviour towards Lady Umm Kulthum (s).

This chapter will attempt to present the argument from various different perspectives analysing the main opinions held amongst both schools of thought. The view from Sunni scholars will be presented first, using the narrations that are accepted by Sunni scholars as proof that the marriage took place. These narrations will then be scrutinised for the validity of the chain of narrators and content of the narration making use of the work of several Shi'a scholars including Ayatollah Syed Ali Milani and Sheikh Abeed Kilbani. After presenting some further arguments refuting the marriage, the view from some Shi'a scholars who accept the marriage took place will be put forward. These scholars use a different group of narrations which explain that the marriage took place under duress. An examination of these narrations will be presented followed by two other possible outcomes to the debate: that Umar did in fact marry a lady named Umm Kulthum, but it was not Lady Umm Kulthum (s), daughter of Lady Fatima (s) and that instead she married her paternal cousin, Aun Ibn Ja'far.

By examining the narrations and using logical arguments, this chapter aims to reach a reasonable conclusion to the debate regarding Lady Umm Kulthum's (s) marriage to Umar. From the evidence, it is my humble opinion that Lady Umm Kulthum (s) did *not* marry Umar al Khattab, but rather that she married her cousin, Aun Ibn Ja'far.

Some Views from Sunni Scholars

Below are two forms of the narration to open the debate on whether the marriage took place. The first tells the story from Umar's perspective, whilst the second is from the perspective of Lady Umm Kulthum (s). Analysing these narrations will establish the basis of the marriage and this will be followed by a discussion on the possibility of the historical validity of the marriage.

From Umar's Perspective

It is narrated: *"She* [Lady Umm Kulthum (s)] *married Umar before she reached puberty and she stayed with Umar until he was killed and bore Zayd and Ruqayya."*

"[Upon approach] *Ali Ibn Abi Talib said to Umar 'I have kept my children for the children of Ja'far (at-Tayyar).' Umar*

replied 'Marry her to me, oh Ali! For I swear there is no one on the face of the earth who is worthier of accompanying her than me' to which Ali replied 'I have (now) done so' agreeing to Umar's request."

"Umar found a group from the emigrants (Muhajireen) sitting between the grave and the pulpit of the Prophet (s) including Ali, Zubayr, Talha, Uthman and Abdul Rahmaan Ibn Awf and stated Congratulate me! Congratulate me!" To which they replied "For what, oh Commander of the Faithful?"

"Umar responded 'For the sake of the daughter of Ali Ibn Abi Talib, for the Prophet has said 'every relation and every cause will be cut off in the hereafter except my relation and my cause.' I used to accompany him and very much wanted to get this merit'"[1].

From Lady Umm Kulthum's (s) Perspective

In response to the approach of Umar, Imam Ali (a) is narrated to have said: *"No, for she is a young girl."* Umar replied *"By Allah! We know, what has that got to do with you? We know what is within you."*

"Lady Umm Kulthum was sent to him. Ali gave her a cloth and stated 'Go to the Commander of the Faithful [Umar]. Say to him my father has sent me and sends you his greetings and says, if you like this cloth you may keep it and if you do not like it you may return it'".

"When this was conveyed to Umar by Lady Umm Kulthum, he responded 'May Allah bless you and your father; tell him we are pleased'. Then Umar married her and she bore his son Zayd"[2]

---

1   al-Baghdadi, Ibn Sa'd, *Tabaqat al-Kubra*, vol. 8, page 463; see also al-Baladhuri, *Ansaab al-Ashraaf*, vol.2, page 411

2   Due to its explicit nature, part of this narration has been omitted from the text to preserve the sanctity of Lady Umm Kulthum's (s) holy

And

It is narrated *"Umar asked Ali for the hand of Umm Kulthum. Ali replied that she was too young. Umar said 'Marry her to me and do as I say for I wish to attain to that position which no one else has attained'. Ali then said, 'I shall send Umm Kulthum to you. If you like her then I shall marry her to you'. Ali then sent the girl with a cloth and told her to say to Umar 'This is the scarf that I was talking about'. She conveyed these words to Umar, who said 'Tell your father that I accept'. Umar then touched the girl's calf. She exclaimed, 'You have done this to me? If it had not been the fact that you were Caliph of the Muslims I would have broken your nose'. The girl went home and repeated the episode to her father, stating 'You sent me to a foul man', with that Ali said 'He is your husband'. Umar then attended a gathering of the emigrants and said 'Congratulate me'. They said 'Why?' He said 'I have married Umm Kulthum, daughter of Ali'"*[1].

AN ANALYSIS OF THESE NARRATIONS

These narrations are from Sunni compilations. There are many other similar narrations, some of which speak quite explicitly about the details of the conversations and interactions before the marriage. The traditions cited are the same texts that each generation of scholar is first introduced to when assessing the authenticity of the marriage between Lady Umm Kulthum (s) and Umar, therefore before analysing any associated issues, it is necessary to inspect these narrations.

personality. For the full narration see: al-Baghdadi, Ibn Sa'd, *Tabaqat al-Kubra*, vol. 8, page 464. Other narrations of this kind can be found in the following sources: al-Khateeb, *Tareekh al-Baghdad*, vol. 6, pages 182-183 and al-Asqalani, Ibn Hajar, *Sawa'iq al-Muhriqa*, page 280.

1 Ibn Abd al-Barr, *al-Istiab fi Ma'rifat al-Ashaab*, vol. 4, page 467

A step by step examination of these narrations will follow. An attempt will be made to demonstrate how these narrations are unacceptable in accordance with the sciences of testing the validity of a narration. Furthermore, it is also important to keep in mind that these narrations may not be acceptable to either school of thought due to the depiction of Umar and Imam Ali (a) in addition to preserving the sanctity of the Prophet's (s) granddaughter.

ANALYSIS OF THE CONTENT

There are several evident and consistent issues that arise from both forms of narrations. The first point of discussion regarding Umar, is that he approached Imam Ali (a) for the hand of Lady Umm Kulthum (s) when she had reached the age of puberty or when she was much younger, as other traditions state that Imam Ali's (a) initial response to Umar was *"No, for she is still a milk fed child"*[1]. This implies that Umar had approached Lady Umm Kulthum (s) when she was not at a suitable age for marriage.

The second point which requires discussion is that Umar appears to have acted inappropriately towards Lady Umm Kulthum (s) in a number of different ways in order to ensure his approval was met. The narrations also mention that Lady Umm Kulthum (s) complained to her father of these acts and that the Imam (a) is reported to have told his daughter to accept Umar as her husband. This is inconsistent with the view of the Imam (a).

The third point regarding Umar's behaviour in these narrations relate to his understanding of the Prophetic tradition which implies that all family ties will be severed on the Day of Judgement, except those of the family of the Prophet (s). According to the Holy Qur'an it is neither

1 al-Baghdadi, Ibn Sa'd, *Tabaqat al-Kubra*, vol. 8, page 464

blood nor relation that is of any value in the eyes of Allah (swt). The example of Prophet Nuh (a) and his son is often cited to illustrate this point. Prophet Nuh (a) was assured by Allah (swt) that his family members would be saved from drowning in the flood. However, as the water rose, Prophet Nuh's (a) son rejected him and refused to join him and the rest of his family in the ark; this resulted in Prophet Nuh's (a) son drowning in the flood. He called out to Allah (swt) *"My son belongs to my family and your promise is true"* to which Allah (swt) responded *"Indeed he is not of your family; he is of evil conduct"* (11:45-46). The example of Prophet Nuh (a) and his son illustrates that even though a person may be part of the family of the Prophet (s), it is their belief and deeds that grant them association to the Prophet (s). This means that even if Umar married Lady Umm Kulthum (s) he would not be granted automatic association with the Prophet (s) as the narration regarding the Day of Judgement relates to those who attach themselves to the Prophet (s) through love, loyalty and obedience. According to these narrations, Umar had a very simplistic understanding of the Prophetic narration.

On the other hand, Sheikh Kilbani raises the point that it is unanimously accepted that Umar was the father-in-law of the Holy Prophet (s) by virtue of his daughter Hafsa's marriage and this is considered to be a significant family tie[1]. One might question why Umar and other companions had overlooked this relation to Holy Prophet (s).

Furthermore, the narration suggests that Imam Ali (a) gave his daughter in marriage on the basis of Umar's desire to be connected to the Ahlul Bayt (a). This would have contradicted the practise (*sunnah*) of the Ahlul Bayt (a). For example, it is narrated that Mu'waiya Ibn Abi Sufyan wanted to be connected to the Banu Hashim (the tribe

---

1 Kilbani, Abeed, *Hal Tazawuj Umar bi Umm Kulthum?* page 4

which the Ahlul Bayt (a) belonged to), through marriage to obtain honour and glory. He wrote to his governor Marwan Ibn Hakam to arrange the marriage of his son Yazid to Zainab the daughter of Abdullah Ibn Ja'far. Marwan approached Imam Hassan (a) who told him to gather the people; members of Banu Umayyah and Banu Hashim attended this gathering. During the gathering, Marwan rose and praised Mu'awiya, lauding him as if he was a prophet, after which Imam Hassan (a) rose, publicly refusing such a marriage, stating *"As for what you have mentioned, we do not turn away from the practice of the Prophet (s). As for reconciling the tribes, we have shown enmity to you for Allah and in Allah, therefore we do not make peace with you for the life in this world. We have seen that we have to marry her (Zainab) to her cousin al-Qasim Ibn Mohammad Ibn Ja'far"*[1].

Imam Hassan (a) refused to marry Zainab the daughter of Abdullah Ibn Ja'far to Mu'awiya, the enemy of the Ahlul Bayt (a). Mu'awiya wanted to be connected to the Ahlul Bayt (a) to elevate his status, but the marriage would have opposed the edict of the Holy Qur'an which states that *"Unclean ones are for unclean things and good things are for good ones"* (24:26). This makes it more unlikely that Imam Ali (a) would have given his own daughter's hand in marriage to Umar, who is considered to be the enemy of the Ahlul Bayt (a) as Imam Hassan (a) would not have opposed his father's practice.

The narrations show Imam Ali (a) initially rejecting Umar's proposal. He is portrayed as someone who is very quickly and easily convinced; he is said to have sent Lady Umm Kulthum (s) to Umar to model a cloth on her father's behalf. Having returned, he tells her of the decision and against his daughter's wishes, marries her to Umar, this is also inconsistent with the known view of Imam Ali (a).

---

1 Qarashi, *The Life of Imam al-Hasan*, pages 574-575

Sheikh Abeed Kilbani presents a different approach to the initial discussion. As mentioned in the chapter entitled 'The Debate Regarding Her Existence' it is clear that there is a strong opinion that Lady Umm Kulthum (s) did not exist or rather that title refers to her elder sister Lady Zainab (s); this belief can also be found in the Sunni schools of thought. Sheikh Kilbani quotes the work of Ibn Hajar Asqalani, a leading Sunni scholar who wrote: "*Those who witnessed (the event concerning) the ownership of Fadak were Ali, Hassanayn and Umm Kulthum*"[1]. Sheikh Kilbani questions: "*Where was Zainab for this witnessing and why would she not participate with her family? Was she not certain about the ownership or was she not available in Medina during the incident? Or does this (tradition) signify that Zainab is the same as Umm Kulthum for it would be against logic to bring the younger daughter but leave the elder*"[2]. The argument raised by Sheikh Kilbani is that if there is no consensus amongst the Sunni scholars as to whether she existed or not, there cannot be agreement amongst Sunni scholars that the marriage took place.

According to some scholars, the traditions cited at the beginning of the section are considered to be reputable and agreed upon as the verification for the marriage of Lady Umm Kulthum (s) to Umar. However, the content of the narrations starkly contradict what is known about the noble characteristics of the first Holy Imam (a). For the Sunni Muslim who upholds the nobility of the second Caliph Umar, the narrations are offensive as they portray him as a man of perverse inclinations and corrupt actions. Neither portrayal would be acceptable to either school of thought. It is for these reasons that I am inclined to reject the content of the narration as evidence for the marriage.

---

1 *as-Sawaiq al-Muhriqa*, page 27

2 Kilbani, Abeed, *Hal Tazawuj Umar bi Umm Kulthum?* page 16

An Analysis of the Chains of Narration

This section aims to assess the quality of the chains of narration (*asnaad*). Although the content of the narration, analysed above, has many flaws, the chain may be sound or even vice versa and thus in the 'science of narrations' both are therefore subject to further scrutiny. When both the content and the chain are scrutinised and found to be problematic, the narration can safely be rejected. This section will refer to the work of Ayatollah Syed Ali Milani, a leading scholar in this field of research.

As the narrations mentioned have been recorded in Sunni compilations, the first area of assessment is to observe the veracity of the traditions according to the standards set by the Sunni scholars themselves. This will allow the reader to appreciate whether the reports should hold a high degree of historical value or whether they should be disregarded as points of reference in the debate.

According to Ayatollah Milani, the primary point of discussion is to note that these narrations were "*found by Imams Bukhari and Muslim[1] but neither included it into their authentic compilations*". He expands on this issue by highlighting that not a single narration regarding the marriage can be found in any of the leading Sunni collections, known as *al-Sihah al-Sittah* or 'the six major narration compilations[2]' stating the traditions are "*not compiled in*

1 Muhammad Ibn Isma'il al-Bukhari (d. 256 AH/870 AD) and Muslim Ibn al-Hajjaj al-Nishapuri (d. 261 AH/857 AD), considered amongst the Sunni Muslims to have compiled the two most authentic collections of narrations.

2 The *Sihah al-Sittah* also includes *Sunan al-Sughra* by Ahmad Ibn Shu'ayb al-Nasa'i (d. 303 AH/915 AD); *Sunan Abu Dawood* by Abu Dawood (d. 275 AH/889 AD); *Jami' al-Tirmidhi* by Muhammad Ibn 'Isa al-Tirmidhi (d. 279 AH/892 AD); *Sunan ibn Majah* by Muhammad Ibn Yazid al-Qazwini (commonly known as Ibn Majah) (d. 273 AH/887 AD). These are deemed the most authentic collections and beyond reproach, but the statement *masaneed mu'tabarah* would

the books focusing on famous chains of narrations (masaneed mu'tabarah)"[1].

This issue is of considerable significance, as it raises questions as to why the six most senior scholars of tradition chose not to include the narrations about the marriage. Furthermore, one might question why the methodology of some scholars of later generations and a lesser repute would find the same traditions worthy of compilation. It is accepted amongst the Sunni scholars, the books which cite the incident are of the secondary or even tertiary category of reliability. Therefore, the absence of the marriage in all the primary collections ultimately throws much doubt on the validity of such traditions.

When assessing the validity of a narration, it is also very important to scrutinise the *chain* of narrators to ensure the reliability of the source. Ayatollah Milani opens this discussion by noting that the names of senior Shi'a personalities can be found in the chain of narrators. He says,"*that which is in this topic is what has been narrated by the Imam's (a) and their followers found in (compilations such as) Tabaqat, al-Mustadrak and Sunan Bayhaqi*". This is a key point to note as one may be inclined to consider the narration as authentic if a member of the Ahlul Bayt (a) and their followers have substantiated or advocated the marriage. However, Ayatollah Milani negates this by questioning the reasons for these names being present in the chain of narration: "*Two important aspects come from this. The first is that we have followed all the texts and found that whenever opponents wanted to attribute something to the Ahlul Bayt (a) – something not pleasing (correct) to them, they have fabricated these (narrations) by the very people who were around the Ahlul Bayt (a)*".

include other primary works such as the *Musnad* of Imam Ahmed Ibn Hanbal (d. 164 AH/780 AD).

1 Milani, A., *Khabr Tazweej Umm Kulthum min Umar*, page 23

It should be noted that Ayatollah Milani is not necessarily criticising the authors of the previously named works. Rather, he is criticising particular groups and personalities in history, who when wanting to feed their own political aspirations, would initiate and circulate fabricated narrations attributed to the Ahlul Bayt (a). Here Ayatollah Milani offers examples such as: "*When they wanted to abuse the Prophet, his daughter and the Commander of the Faithful they made the story that Ali (a) wanted to marry the daughter of Abu Jahl. When they wanted to fabricate the merits of the companions such as 'my companions are like stars, whomsoever you follow, you will be guided' they attributed this to Imam Ja'far as-Sadiq (a)*". Ayatollah Milani's point is that the results of such narrations are that they would eventually become eternalised in the annals of compilations but one must also have the foresight to examine which groups might benefit from such traditions in order to conclude their true value.

The second area of Ayatollah Milani's assessment of the chains of narration addresses the veracity of individuals who narrate the tradition. He states "*They have narrated this (the marriage) in (the book) Tabaqat* [by Ibn Sa'd al-Baghdadi] *from Imam's Ja'far as-Sadiq and Mohammed Baqir and in (the book) al-Mustadrak from Imam's as-Sadiq, Baqir and Zain al-Abideen*"[1]. However, Ayatollah Milani questions Ibn Sa'd al-Baghdadi's choice of narrators in *Tabaqat* and thus his credibility too. He states that Ibn Sa'd has "*violated the dignity of Imam Ja'far as-Sadiq (a) by saying: 'He used to narrate a lot of traditions; he cannot be taken as a proof and is a weak narrator'*"[2].

This view of Imam as-Sadiq (a) is not an uncommon

---

1   He mentions similar points for the books *Dhurriat at-Taahira* and *Sunan al-Bayhaqi*

2   Milani, A., *Khabr Tazweej Umm Kulthum min Umar*, page 24

among Sunni scholars of tradition. Due to exaggerated praises and false beliefs attributed to Imam as-Sadiq (a) "*Mohammed Ibn Isma'il Bukhari, who travelled to far-away places such as Balkh, Baghdad, Basra, Kufa, Damascus and Asqalan in order to gather hadith reports, did not relate even one hadith in his Sahih Bukhari on the authority of Imam Sadiq (a)*"[1].

The point being raised by Ayatollah Milani is an important one. He highlights a contradiction that the foremost Sunni scholars do not take narrations from Imam as-Sadiq (a) as reliable on matters such as jurisprudence and philosophy, but yet they accept these reported narrations on the subject of the marriage. Ayatollah Milani uses this argument to support his previous point that if Imam as-Sadiq (a) is considered as a weak narrator from the Sunni perspective but infallible from the Shi'a, the narration could only serve a politically driven agenda to attribute such a narration to the Imam (a) in order to establish a point of incongruity among the Shi'a community.

In addition to this, Ayatollah Milani then lists more than a dozen individuals all of whom appear within the chain of narrators of these texts and offers evidence from Sunni books of *rijaal* explaining why they are considered to be weak narrators thus discrediting the entire group of narrations regarding the marriage[2].

---

1 Najafabadi, Salehi, *Religious Extremism*, pages 100-101. For further information on the issues attributed to Imam Sadiq (a) and their effects see pages 97-109, 128-130 and 145-150 of the same book.

2 Milani, A., *Khabr Tazweej Umm Kulthum min Umar*, pages 25-41

Further Arguments Refuting The Marriage

The issues raised are sufficient evidence to reject the authenticity of these narrations and therefore to deny that the marriage took place. Yet, scholars have mentioned more than thirty additional arguments to support the view that the marriage did not take place. Some of these include:

1) If it is agreed that Umar had caused the death of Lady Fatima (s), how could Imam Ali (a) sanction the marriage of her daughter to the man that killed her mother?

2) If Lady Fatima (s) died whilst being angry with Umar, his marrying her daughter would have angered her further; Imam Ali (a) would not disregard the sentiments of the daughter of the Prophet (s).

3) If Lady Umm Kulthum (s) was at a marriageable age, she was not of equivalent maturity to Umar, thus acting contrary to the prophetic practice.

4) If Lady Umm Kulthum (s) was at a marriageable age, she was not of equivalent social status to Umar; being from Banu Hashim inclined her to marrying from Banu Hashim.

5) There is no narration supporting the recitation of a marriage formula or marriage event taking place, despite being two of the famous households in Islam.

6) Lady Zainab al-Kubra, the elder daughter of Imam Ali (a) was not married at this time; why would Umar have approached the younger sister and not the elder one and similarly why would Imam Ali (a) have authorised the marriage of the younger daughter and not the elder?

Some Views from Shi'a Scholars

Despite these arguments there are renowned scholars from the Shi'a school of thought that authenticate the marriage of Lady Umm Kulthum (s) to Umar al-Khattab; these include:

i) **Syed Murtadha Allama al-Huda**
Kitab as-Shafee, vol. 3, page 272
Wa Tanzeehil Ambiyaa, page 191
Wal Majmoo'atul Thalitha, vol. 3, pages 149-150

ii) **Sheikh Muhammad Ibn Ya'qub al-Kulayni**
Al-Kafi, vol. 5, page 346

iii) **Allama al-Kufi**
Al-Istighatha, pages 80-82

iv) **Qadhi al-No'man**
Sharh al-Akbaar, vol. 2, page 507

v) **Sheikh Muhammad Ibn Hassan at-Tusi**
Tamheed al-Usul wal Iqtisaad, pages 386-387

vi) **Sheikh Fadhl Ibn Hasan at-Tabrasi**
I'ilaam al-Wara, vol. 1, page 397

vii) **Allama Mohammad Baqir Majlisi**
Mir'at al-Uqool, vol. 20, page 42

The reasons for their belief that the marriage between Lady Umm Kulthum (s) and Umar took place are not based on the Sunni narrations cited above. They are based on traditions found in Shi'a books which have offered a different perspective on the marriage. An example of this is reported from Imam as-Sadiq (a), he is narrated to have said: *"When Umar sought the hand of Umm Kulthum for marriage, Ali said 'but she is only a child'. Umar said to al-Abbas 'I sought the hand of the daughter of your nephew and he turned me down. By Allah, I shall damage the well of Zamzam and I shall leave nothing precious belonging to you except that I shall ruin it and I shall get two witnesses to testify that he stole and I shall cut off his right hand.' Al-Abbas came and informed Ali of what Umar had said asking him to let him take care of that matter, which he did*[1]. Imam as-Sadiq (a) is also narrated to have said *"That was a womb which was taken from us by force"*[2].

These two traditions are of great value in this discussion because they attempt to explain how Shi'a scholars reconcile that marriage took place when Imam Ali (a) agreed to the marriage after having initially refused Umar's request. The first tradition by Imam as-Sadiq (a) describes Umar's reaction to the rejection. He approached one of the most influential family members and a sincere companion to the Holy Prophet (s). He then issued a series of threats that would result in a blockade against the Ahlul Bayt (a) and the Muslim nation, considering Imam Ali (a) as a criminal punished by the state. Thus the scholars who hold the position that the marriage took place, consider it to have been under compulsion. Their statements include:

"Even if the marriage did take place, it was an apparent marriage. The Commander of the Faithful was forced. He allowed the marriage to stop the bloodshed"[3].

And

"When Umar asked for the hand of Lady Umm Kulthum, Ali thought to himself: 'If I say no, those things would occur which the Prophet (s) tried to prevent and for which reason

---

1 al-Kulayni, Mohammed Ya'qub, *al-Kafi*, vol. 5, the chapter entitled 'The Marriage of Umm Kulthum', page 346

2 Ibid

3 Hamadani, Ahmad Rahmani, *Fatima Zahra Bahjatu Qalbi Mustapha*, pages 654-655

he asked me to exercise patience, which is that people will fall into apostasy.' Thus, it was better to hand over Lady Umm Kulthum to him"[1].

And

"As for Umm Kulthum, she is the one whom Umar Ibn al-Khattab married. Our associates say that Ali only married her to him after putting up a lot of resistance, strong refusals and finding any excuse he could. Ultimately he was forced by circumstances to turn her matter over to Abbas Ibn 'Abd al-Muttalib who married her off"[2].

AN ANALYSIS OF THESE NARRATIONS

The narrations describe Umar as threatening and forceful which is in keeping with the Shi'a perspective of his personality. Furthermore, the narrations are found in reputable books of traditions and explain the previously ambiguous issue of Imam Ali's (a) change of stance. For these reasons, a further investigation into the nature of these traditions is important to conclude whether the marriage took place.

The first area of analysis is to inspect the reliability of the chain of narrators (*sanad*). The narration in which Imam as-Sadiq (a) is said to have stated Lady Umm Kulthum (s) *"was taken by force"* is recorded from *"Ali Ibn Ibrahim, who heard from his father, who heard from the son of the father of Umayr, who heard from Hisham Ibn Salim, from Hammad who heard from Zurarah"* narrating from Imam Ali (a).

This chain includes some of the most famous and trusted names of Shi'a narrators. For example the narrations of Hisham, Ali Ibn Ibrahim and his father can be

1 al-Kufi, *Al-Istighatha*, page 80
2 at-Tabrasi, *I'ilaam al-Wara*, vol. 1, page 397

found literally thousands of times in the compilations of Sheikh al-Kulayni and Allama Majlisi; this indicates that scholars separated by several generations found no alternative view on their trustworthiness. The tradition emanates from Zurarah, a companion who is of the most outstanding character. For example it is narrated Imam as-Sadiq (a) said about Zurarah and other companions like him that they are "*the tent pegs of the world*" and "*the protectors of the religion, confidants of my father and the repositories of my secrets*"[1]. The scholars of *rijal* have labelled him "*A great reciter of Qur'an, a high jurist, an excellent speaker, eloquent and trustworthy*"[2].

Despite its brevity the content of the narration has also undergone much scrutiny. The word farj has been translated here as "womb (which was taken)". However, there are some who have translated the word literally to mean the private parts of a woman, leading the tradition to imply something quite specific. There are many contemporary researchers who have suggested that this would be a vulgar statement by Imam as-Sadiq (a) and considering Lady Umm Kulthum (s) would be the great aunt of the Imam (a), this is not a statement in keeping with his purified tongue. Therefore one would be inclined to reject the narration based on its content. As the point is that the Imam (a) would never use vulgar language, let alone about his noble aunt, if the narration is to be accepted, this translation must be discarded as inaccurate. When Al-lama Majlisi addressed this issue he said that the word farj should be translated as 'honour'[3] altering the translation to: "that was an honour which was taken from us by force". This translation is in keeping with the language of the Holy

---

1   Takim, Liyakat, *The Heirs of the Prophet*, pages 81-82
2   Kho'i, A., *Mu'jam al-Rijaal al-Hadith*, vol. 8, pages 225-227
3   al-Majlisi, *Bihar al-Anwar*, vol. 42, pages 106-109

Qur'an which uses the word in a similar context: "*And Maryam, the daughter of Imraan who guarded her chastity, so We breathed into her of Our inspiration*" (66:12) and "*Mention the one who guarded her chastity, so We breathed into her of Our inspiration*" (21:91). Another understanding of the word farj – or honour, is derived from applying its metaphorical meaning. In spoken Arabic, the word farj was often used in place of the word 'ird being the direct female relatives of a man, such as his mother, wife or sisters and thus not a particular body part or title.

If it is assumed that Imam as-Sadiq (a) was not under any dissimulation (*taqiyyah*) when recounting this issue, it is possible he could have been expressing his anguish at the situation and responding to the actual *circulation* of such audacious narrations and not the event itself.

In this case, it is part of the honour of the Imam (a) that his daughters married the sons of his brother. Moreover, one might argue that even the idea of the marriage of his daughter to the one implicated in her mother's death would have grieved him tremendously and thus extending to Imam as-Sadiq (a) too. Knowing this, one might argue further that if the Imam (a) had heard of these narrations, his response might have been the same words but contextualised by the circumstance. The narration can therefore be retranslated to suggest that "(the very spreading of this idea of the marriage has resulted in) that honour being taken from us by force".

Just as with the narrations describing the approach of Umar, the scholars of polemics have found thirty reasons for the weakness of this narration[1] of which two are: firstly, that the text states Imam as-Sadiq (a) mentioned Umm Kulthum was taken by force, but this does not identify

---

1 For a full list, see article: Answering-Ansar, *Nikah of Lady Umme Kulthum*, pages 59-78

which Umm Kulthum the Imam (a) is referring to; as this was a common name during that era, the narration cannot be considered to definitely refer to the daughter of Lady Fatima (s). Secondly, just as verification is needed of which person was taken by force, the narration also fails to identify *the person* who performed the action. If the narration does not name Umar as the person enforcing the action, the tradition cannot be said to refer to Umar.

It appears the issue of determining which Umm Kulthum is being referred to in the Shi'a texts is not confined to this example. Proponents of the marriage highlight another narration as evidence that the marriage took place. They cite the narration that Imam as-Sadiq (a) was asked concerning a woman whose husband has died: "*can she see out her Iddah[1] period in her house or wherever she wants*" he replied "*it is wherever she wants; Ali (a) brought Umm Kulthum to his house when Umar died and she became free*"[2].

As the subsequent section argues, there are many traditions recording the marriage of Umar and Umm Kulthum, daughter of Abu Bakr, who later became the adopted daughter of Imam Ali (a). Consequently, the ambiguity surrounding the identity of the named Umm Kulthum in these traditions becomes an imperative factor, therefore one cannot assume whom the narration is referring to.

Furthermore, these traditions do not conclude with certainty that Imam Ali (a) married his daughter to Umar. The verse of Qur'an concerning the issue of *iddah* states: "*And those of you who die and leave wives behind (should make) a bequest in favour of their wives' maintenance for a*

---

1 The period of waiting for a woman that must be observed after the death of her spouse or after divorce

2 al-Kulayni, *al-Kafi*, Kitab al-Talaq, vol 6 page 115. The tradition is also narrated as:"*Ali came to Umm Kulthum, took her hand and sent her to his house*", Milani, A., *Khabr Tazweej Umm Kulthum min Umar*, page 59

year without turning (them) out; then if they themselves go away there is no blame on you" (2:240). The verse offers two sequential possibilities. The first possibility is that the wives should remain under the financial aid and location of their husband's house. However, if they choose to leave there is no blame on them. Nonetheless, the tradition does not clarify why Imam Ali (a) acted on the second option before exercising the first. This inconsistency renders the content of the narration unacceptable and not in keeping with the view of the Imam (a).

The remaining tradition citing Umar's series of threats also fails to provide sufficient evidence for the marriage. The narrations above clearly state that due to Umar's threats insisting on the marriage, Imam Ali (a) put the matter in the hands of Abbas (a). However, nowhere does it state that the marriage was a consequence of this action by Imam Ali (a). Moreover, this tradition can be used as an argument to strengthen a case that the marriage did not materialise as Abbas (a) was given authority over the matter leaving Umar's threats to Imam Ali (a) entirely futile.

This perspective is corroborated by Imam as-Sadiq (a) in a narration stating: *"People claim that Ali married his daughter to such a person!" The Imam, who was until then sitting down, stood up and angrily said "Whoever holds such a viewpoint is misled. Glory be to Allah! Was Imam Ali unable to free his daughter from their clutches? He could have stood between them and her to protect her; they have fabricated a lie!"*[1].

The narrations from the Shi'a texts have distinctive features compared to the Sunni texts on the issue of the marriage. Whilst both the text and chain of the Sunni texts have clear grounds for rejection, the quality of the chains of narration in the Shi'a text are faultless. However,

1 al-Mulk , M.T., Lisan, *Nasihk al-Tawarikh*, vol. 3 page 408

an analysis of their content in this section has proved ambiguous especially when discerning which personalities are being referred to. Moreover, the scholars who argue that the marriage took place under duress have not mentioned or examined these flaws.

As the authenticity of the chains of narration are irrefutable and their content is unanimous in claiming a lady named Umm Kulthum from the household of Ali (a) was married to Umar it can be concluded that this broad fact is true, However, the question still remains unanswered about whether this Umm Kulthum is the daughter of Lady Fatima (s). The next section offers a suggestion as to whom the above narrations could be referring to.

Umm Kulthum bint Abu Bakr

One of the central issues of the debate is that the marriage of Umar to Umm Kulthum is so widely narrated in biographies and historical accounts, from both the Sunni and the Shi'a, that scholars have become adamant that a marriage did take place. As mentioned, it remains ambiguous whether the Umm Kulthum referred to is in fact Lady Umm Kulthum (s) daughter of Lady Fatima (s). Therefore, it becomes necessary to offer an investigation into other possible identities of the Umm Kulthum that married Umar.

Historical sources indicate that Umar was married to several ladies with the title of Umm Kulthum, including:

i)   Umm Kulthum Jameela bint Asim bin Thabit[1]

ii) Umm Kulthum bint Jarweela Khuzeema[2]

---

1   Bakari, Hussain Diyar, *Tareekh Khamees*, vol. 2, page 251
2   Ibn Athir, *al-Kamil fi Tareekh*, vol. 3, page

iii) Umm Kulthum bint Ukba bin Abi Mayyath[1]

iv) Umm Kulthum bint Rahab[2]

The difference between the ladies mentioned above and the Umm Kulthum mentioned in the Sunni books (and some Shi'a books) is that she was the daughter of Imam Ali (a) and specifically of young age, whilst none of the ladies mentioned above bear those resemblances, therefore excluding them from being reconciled as the true identity of the Umm Kulthum in question. There is however, one other wife of Umar bearing these qualities and she was Umm Kulthum daughter of Abu Bakr, the first Caliph and close companion of Umar. According to narrations she was born to Asma bint Umays in the 12th year of *hijrah* just after the death of Abu Bakr, her father, following which, historians agree, Asma married Imam Ali (a) making this Umm Kulthum his step-daughter[3].

The narrations from the Sunni books are replete with narrations of an approach from Umar toward Umm Kulthum daughter of Abu Bakr. These include: "*Umar proposed to marry Umm Kulthum bint Abu Bakr and made the proposal to A'isha. A'isha replied 'She is too young, but then where we will she go without you?' Umm Kulthum approached A'isha and said 'I have heard that you want to marry me to Umar. He will give me a tough life; I am in need of a young man, who loves this world. If you marry me to Umar then I shall complain before Rasulullah.' A'isha then summoned Amr Ibn Aas who said 'I shall deal with the matter'. Amr spoke to Umar, after a general conversation he said 'I hear that you*

1 Qasthalani, *Sharh Sahih al-Bukhari*, vol. 4, page 349

2 Article: Answering-Ansar team, *Nikah of Lady Umme Kulthum*, page 43 (Quoted from *Sunan Abu Dawud* and *Sunan Ibn Majah*)

3 at-Tabari, *Tareekh at-Tabari*, vol. 2, page 50; see also Bakari, Hussain Diyar, *Tareekh Khamees*, vol. 2, page 267

intend on marrying'. Umar replied 'Yes'. Amr Ibn Aas asked 'Who?' Umar replied 'Umm Kulthum bint Abu Bakr'. Amr then said 'She is a child that shall cry for her father every day'. Umar then said 'Did A'isha send you?"[1].

These traditions appear to explain a number of un-answered or ambiguous issues including: the identity of which Umm Kulthum was approached; her tender age; why Imam Ali (a) initially refused the advance citing his children have been kept for the children of Ja'far at-Tayyar but was then convinced otherwise and why Imam (a) returned Umm Kulthum back to his house after Umar's death. As the tradition also mentions the involvement and close relationship of A'isha, also a daughter of Abu Bakr and thus sister to Umm Kulthum, it adds a significant weight to the perspective that the approach was in fact to Umm Kulthum bint Abu Bakr, who was under the guardi-anship of Imam Ali (a).

The great Ayatollah Mar'ashi Najafi proposed this opinion when he wrote: "*It should be known that the Umm Kulthum that was married by the second Caliph was the daughter of Asma bint Umays and the sister of Mohammed Ibn Abi Bakr. Her name was Rabeeba and she was raised by the Commander of the Faithful, Ali and thus was not his daughter as it is famously known by the historians and scholars of tradition. We have completed the research about this fact*"[2].

---

1 al-Hindi, *Kanz al-Ummal*, vol. 7, page 98. For similar narrations, see: Ibn Kathir, *al-Bidaya wan-Nihaya* vol. 7, page 139; Ibn Athir, *al-Kamil fi Tareekh* vol. 3, page 27 and at-Tabari, *Tareekh at-Tabari*, vol. 5, page 273. See also Ibn Asakir, *Tareekh Dimishq*, vol. 25, page 96

2 Najafi, Shahabuddin Mara'shi, *Sharh Ihqaq al-Haqq*, (addressing the issues of vol. 2 page 376), vol. 3, page 315

Lady Umm Kulthum and Aun ibn Ja'far

One of the commonly reported details of the conversation between Umar and Imam Ali (a) is the Imam's (a) response: "*I kept my children for the children of Ja'far (at-Tayyar)*" or "*our children are for the children of Ja'far (at-Tayyar)*". In this light it is established that Lady Zainab (s) daughter of Lady Fatima (s) married Abdullah Ibn Ja'far. Moreover, an example cited previously in this chapter portrays Imam Hassan (a) continuing this precedent.

If Imam Ali (a) responded with this objection when Umar approached Umm Kulthum daughter of Abu Bakr and later allowed the marriage to take place, it could be argued that he did not pursue his initial assertion as he was only the guardian of Umm Kulthum. Furthermore, there are many traditions which report that Lady Umm Kulthum (s), married Aun Ibn Ja'far (the brother of Abdullah)[1]. It is said that he was martyred, like his father, at the Battle of Tustar during the Caliphate of Umar. From these narrations, it seems that Lady Umm Kulthum (s) did not marry again. This also explains why she did not have a son to offer as a sacrifice on the day of Ashura.

This tradition is considered influential by virtue of its presence in the book *al-Faqih*. Sheikh as-Sadooq, the author, is known as *Ra'is al-Muhaditheen* (The Crown of the Narrators) due to his diligence and proximity to the period of occultation. In addition, the book is also considered in the quartet of primary Shi'a texts which also includes al-Kafi. Therefore, due to the fact that this narration offers a decisive perspective on the marriage whilst the latter does not, it supersedes other texts in any comparison.

1 al-Khafajee, *Maqatil al-Ma'sumeen*, page 307; see also, Sadooq, *Man La Yahdhuruhul Faqih*, vol. 3, page 393

Conclusion

It is very rare for a historical debate to offer such a vast spectrum of perspectives and possible conclusions.

The Sunni stance has been formulated by the scholars of history (*mu'arrikheen*) as oppose to scholars of tradition (*muhadditheen*) and this difference has determined the group of texts adopted. The scholars of history have confined the debate to an inferior group of texts not considered authentic, which materialised some generations after the initial rejection of the marriage by the 'authenticated' texts. Additionally, the subject has not been reassessed or challenged by the mainstream or subsequent generations of scholars. This has resulted in an inability to present contemporary arguments within the discussion, with numerous flaws remaining unanswered. From this perspective, the issue has remained stagnated for the purpose of belying any rift between the Ahlul Bayt (a) and Umar.

The Shi'a viewpoint however, has divided the opinions of the lead scholars since the inception of the debate spanning an entire millennium. What is fascinating to note is the apparent migration of popular belief from the earlier scholars who argued that Umar's marriage was to Lady Umm Kulthum (s) daughter of Lady Fatima (s) specifically under duress, to the stance of contemporary scholars who hold that the identity of the one who married Umar is that of Umm Kulthum daughter of Abu Bakr. This scenario may be due to the earlier generation of scholars who relied on a singular group of texts while the latter used additional evidences from other sources.

The results of these differing narrations and opinions have led to eight possible answers to the controversy over who Lady Umm Kulthum (s) married[1]. These include:

---

1 In order to be concise, not all the traditions regarding these possible

1. She did not exist and therefore could not have married

2. She married Umar and bore his children

3. The marriage to Umar was forced and did not result in children

4. Imam Ali (a) married a *jinni* woman to Umar in place of Lady Umm Kulthum (s)

5. She married Umar, but did not marry others after his death

6. Lady Umm Kulthum (s) married Umar and others after his death

7. She was married to Aun Ibn Ja'far only

8. She married Aun Ibn Ja'far and others after his martyrdom

From these potential outcomes, the three most commonly agreed possibilities are that: the marriage to Umar was genuine; the marriage to Umar was forced; or that Lady Umm Kulthum (s) married Aun Ibn Ja'far.

Having assessed the debates presented above, it is my humble opinion that Lady Umm Kulthum (s) did not marry Umar, the second Caliph, but instead married Aun, the son of Ja'far who was Lady Umm Kulthum's (s) paternal cousin. What follows is justification for this conclusion.

Firstly, the evidence for the marriage to Umar, be it genuine or forced, still relies on the indeterminate traditions of Umar's aggressive approach, Imam Ali's (a) rejections and relying on the shameful texts citing the issues of Umm Kulthum's age. For this reason, it is difficult for scholars of either sect to endorse or defend the marriage using these narrations.

---

outcomes have been mentioned as they are considered to be irrelevant or weak arguments

What is evident from both the Sunni and Shi'a texts regarding Lady Umm Kulthum's (s) marriage to Umar is that there is no possibility to determine for certain that the marriage took place as both sets of texts have an indefinite number of flaws to them; although one may reach a conclusion based upon deduction and reasoning it may be impossible to assert certainty on the matter.

This leaves us with the possibility that Lady Umm Kulthum (s) married Aun ibn Ja'far. There are at least two agreed elements of this debate; firstly that Imam Ali (s) set a precedent of marriage within Ahlul Bayt (a) and numerous traditions recount a marriage to Aun Ibn Ja'far. From the perspective of finding *certainty*, whilst all other aspects lead toward ambiguity one may be inclined to subscribe to the view of this being Lady Umm Kulthum's (s) true and only marriage in keeping with her sanctity and the prevalent contemporary schools of thought. Indeed Allah (swt) knows best.

Beyond the primary aspect of the marriage, this topic is a gift from the legacies of Lady Umm Kulthum (s). From the perspective of the scholar, the breadth of opinions and intricacies of the argument, requires close attention. The debate therefore forms an excellent training ground in the sciences of narration, history, comparative study (*istidlaal*) and biographies. For the masses it also introduces these topics and exposes an element of the level of scrutiny a scholar must apply when addressing a single issue. If the debate itself does not offer certainty, it certainly yields an excellent means of development for all levels of the reading community.

Lady Umm Kulthum during the life of Imam Hassan

The Patient Teacher

The period of Imam Hassan's (a) leadership of the Muslim nation lasted approximately seven months and was fraught with difficult circumstances, including a major attempt on his life[1]. Eventually, he was forced to enter into a peace treaty with Mu'awiya to save the Muslim nation. The Ahlul Bayt (a) supported this strategy; Imam Hussain (a) said *"My brother is true in his actions. All of you should stay home as long as Mu'awiya is alive"*[2]. This recommendation also applied to Lady Umm Kulthum (s). Mu'awiya's ruthlessness was notorious; through her bravery she had defended the rights of the Ahlul Bayt (a) during the time of her noble father, but under these circumstances, they faced grave danger and so Lady Umm Kulthum (s) mirrored her father's patience in these difficult times.

She spent her time peacefully teaching others about the religion of her grandfather, just as Imam Hassan (a)

1 al-Baladhuri, *Ansaab al-Ashraaf*, vol. 3, page 54

2 Ibn Qutaybah, *al-Imamah wa Siyasah*, vol. 1, page 187

had instructed, "*teach others your knowledge and learn new knowledge from others*"[1].

After the abdication of Imam Hassan (a) from the position of Caliph, the family of the Prophet (s) returned back to Medina to continue guiding the people and observing the conditions of the peace treaty. Lady Umm Kulthum (s), who had been the princess of Kufa, returned to her home and remembered the period of prosperity during the lifetime of her grandfather but also the terrible oppression against her mother and father.

The hatred of Mu'awiya towards Imam Hassan (a) had not subsided. He plotted against the Imam (a), manipulating the Imam's (a) own wife, Ju'dah bint Ash'ath, to poison him[2]. A physician was brought to Imam Hassan (a). On seeing his condition, the physician turned to the family members and said "*the poison has cut his bowels into pieces*"[3].

Lady Umm Kulthum (s) and the family gathered around the Imam (a) to spend the last hours with him. Her brother turned to them and described the severe suffering he was facing, saying "*I have been given poison several times but I have never been given poison like this. A part of my liver has come out of my mouth and I began to turn it over with a stick I had*"[4].

Imam Hussain (a) began to weep profusely. Imam Hassan (a) asked why, he replied "*I am weeping due to what has been done to you*". Imam Hassan (a) gathered some strength and responded "*I have been given poison and I will be killed with it, however there is no day like your day, oh father of Abdullah! Thirty thousand people will approach you; they will claim to belong to the nations of our grandfather*

1 al-Majlisi, *Bihar al-Anwar*, vol. 78, page 111

2 al-Mas'udi, *Muruj ad-Dhahab*, vol. 2, page 353

3 Ibn Kathir, *al-Bidaya wan-Nihaya*, vol. 8, page 43

4 Ibid, page 43

and follow the religion. They will gather together to kill you, shed your blood, violate your sacredness, take your progeny and your women as prisoners of war and plunder you"[1]. As the hours passed and the pain intensified, Imam Hassan (a) bequeathed his will to his brother: "*Oh Hussain, as to those whom I have left behind from among my family, my children and your household [I entrust them to you]. Pardon their wrongdoings and accept their doing of good, that you may be a successor and father to them*"[2].

Lady Umm Kulthum (s) was present when her brother was martyred. He joined the ranks of her grandfather, mother and father, all of whom she had witnessed leave this world. Throughout her life, Lady Umm Kulthum (s) had witnessed the enmity of the people towards her family and the oppression they had faced, but this had only served to strengthen her patience and fortitude. All this was to prepare her for the greatest trial of all on the plains of Kerbala, the streets of Damascus, and the court of Yazid.

---

1 al-Majlisi, *Bihar al-Anwar*, vol. 10, page 123

2 al-Amin, M., *A'yaan ash-Shi'a*, vol. 4, page 79

Lady Umm Kulthum During the life of Imam Hussain and Beyond

Fortitude through Adversity

The family of the Prophet (s) continued to protect the religion of Allah (swt) and the wider interest of the Muslim nation after the death of Imam Hassan (a). They turned to Imam Hussain (a) for guidance in this delicate political situation. Imam Hussain (a) decided to observe all aspects of the treaty with Mu'awiya; he spent his time teaching and guiding the people to enjoin good and forbid evil.

When Mu'awiya died in 60 AH, nine years after the death of Imam Hassan (a), he had appointed his son Yazid as the Caliph, contrary to the conditions of the peace treaty.

Amongst the first things that Yazid sought was the allegiance of Imam Hussain (a). In one letter to the governor of Medina, he wrote *"When this letter reaches you, summon al-Hussain Ibn Ali and Abdullah Ibn Zubayr. Take allegiance from them. If they refuse strike off their heads and bring them to me and then take allegiance from the rest of the people thus if anyone refuses, apply the same order to him as applied to al-Hussain and az-Zubayr"*[1].

The Imam (a) replied: *"We are the household of the Prophet, the source of Messengership and the place of descent for the angels. Through us, had Allah begun showering His blessings and with us has He perfected His favours. Yazid is a sinful person, a drunkard, a killer of innocent people and one who openly indulges in sinful acts. A person like me can never pledge allegiance to a person like him"*[2]. This incident marked the dawn of Imam Hussain's (a) revolution; the Ahlul Bayt (a) were no longer safe in the city of the Prophet (s), and they were forced to leave their home.

This chapter is dedicated to relating the series of events surrounding the martrydom of Imam Hussain (a) from Lady Umm Kulthum's (s) perspective. Narrations which mention her, or have been narrated by her have been collected and presented below to demonstrate the crucial role she played in one of the most important events in Islamic history.

Leaving Medina

When the Imam (a) decided to leave Medina and take refuge in Makkah, the ladies of the family were terrified because they had heard of the numerous reports about the imminent tragedy from the Messenger of Allah and thus they all gathered in an atmosphere of sorrow and trepidation. They began to wail and the sounds of their weeping penetrated their surroundings. It was a scene of fear and shock[3]. Their hearts became filled with pain and they said *"Why shouldn't we weep and wail? This day is like the day of the passing away of the Prophet, Ali, Fatima and Has-*

1 Ya'qubi, Ahmed, *Tareekh al-Ya'qubi*, vol. 2, page 241

2 Ibn Tawus, *Maqtal al-Hussain*, page 10-11

3 *Ad-Dar'ul Masluk fi Ahwaal al-Ambiya wal Awsiya*, vol. 1, page 107

san! May the Almighty Allah make us a sacrifice for you, Oh beloved of the righteous!"*[1]. When night fell al-Hussain left Medina accompanied by his two sisters Lady Zainab (s) and Lady Umm Kulthum (s).

Imam Hussain (a) and the close members of his family, including Lady Umm Kulthum (s), left Medina with a small group of followers, and headed toward Makkah.

Lady Umm Kulthum (s) prepared herself for a journey that would be the ultimate test of her bravery and patience; the journey that was foreseen by her grandfather and would end with the brutal martyrdom of her brother, Imam Hussain (a), the plundering of his property and her imprisonment.

Leaving Makkah

Whilst in Makkah, the Imam (a) received thousands of letters from the Shi'a in Kufa who pledged their loyalty to him and promised to support him against the tyrant Yazid[2]. When the Imam's (a) life was in danger in Makkah, he left the sanctified precincts of the holy city and headed towards Kufa.

Imam Hussain (a) departed from his brother Muhammad al-Hanafiya by telling him: *"Know that I have not risen in order to spread evil, nor to show off, nor out of making mischief nor out of oppression; rather I have risen in order to fight for the sole purpose of seeking reform in the nation of my grandfather, the Messenger of Allah, may Allah's peace and blessings be upon him and his family. I want to enjoin good and forbid evil and guide the affairs of the people as my grandfather and father Ali Ibn Abi Talib did"*[3].

---

1 al-Mas'udi, *Muruj ad-Dhahab*, vol. 3, page 54
2 al-Qarashi, *The Life of Imam Hussain*, pages 476-485 and 511-603
3 al-Khawarizmi, *Maqtal al-Hussain*, pages 188-189

But Ubaydallah Ibn Ziyad had threatened and tricked the people of Kufa to abandon the Imam (a) and his supporters. Muslim Ibn Aqil, the Imam's (a) cousin and representative was killed in Kufa. The army of Yazid rode out to meet Imam Hussain (a) and his caravan in the desert; they met in a land called Kerbala.

Arriving at Kerbala

Imam Hussain (a) embedded a spear into the sand beneath him and said *"Here will be the resting place of our animals. Here will be the place where our tents are erected. Here is the place where our blood will flow, where our women will become captives, where our children will become orphans and will be scattered across the plains. We will be buried here and from here we will be raised on the Day of Resurrection"*[1].

Lady Umm Kulthum (s) came to Imam Hussain (a), and said *"Dear brother! This wilderness is frightful. I feel troubled and ill at ease with great fear in my heart"*. The Imam (a) looked at her and said *"Dear sister! When we advanced with our father to the battleground of Siffin we rested at this very place. Our father placed his head in the lap of our brother al-Hassan and slept for a while. I was present as he awoke and began to weep. Al-Hassan asked, 'Oh father! Why do you cry?' Our father replied, 'I have seen this desert in a dream as if it had become a sea of blood and al-Hussain was drowning inside it calling for help without anyone responding'. Then our father turned to me and said, 'Oh Hussain! What will you do when faced with such an event?' I replied that I would persevere with patience"*[2].

---

1 al-Khawarizmi, *Maqtal al-Hussain*. Quoted in: Ishtihardi, M., *Lamentations II*, page 33
2 Ibid

The Eve of Ashura

On the eve of the 10th of Muharram, 61 AH, the army of Umar Ibn Sa'ad advanced toward the camp of Imam Hussain (a). The Imam (a) requested that the battle be postponed to the following morning so that he and his companions could spend the night in prayer and preparation for martyrdom.

Imam Zain al-Abideen (a) said: *"I heard my father on the night preceding the day on which he was killed, as he was mending his sword, reciting some poetry:*

> *Oh Time! Shame on you for a friend!*
> *How many do you have, at dawn and at dusk*
> *Of friends and of vengeance seekers*
> *While time with a substitute is never pleased?*
> *But the affair is with the Mighty One*
> *And every living being will go His way*

He repeated the verse twice or thrice; therefore I understood his implication, so I was overcome with tears, yet I remained silent knowing that fate was near. As for my aunt Zainab, once she heard those verses, she leapt and went to see him. She said to him 'Woe unto me! Shall I survive you?! I wish death had deprived me of life! My mother Fatima has just died followed by my father Ali then my brother al-Hassan'"[1]. The women wept when they saw her weeping, beating their cheeks. Lady Umm Kulthum (s) cried out *"Oh Muhammad! Oh Ali! Oh mother! Oh Hussain! How lost we are after you!"* Imam Hussain (a) said, *"Oh sister! Oh Umm Kulthum! Oh Fatima! Oh Rubab! Pay attention to me. Once I am killed, you should not tear your pockets nor scratch your cheeks nor*

---

1 at-Tabari, *Tareekh at-Tabari*, vol. 4, page 240; see also al-Khawarizmi, *Maqtal al-Hussain*, vol. 1 page 238

utter any verbal abuse"[1].

Nafi' Ibn Hilal narrates the Imam (a) went to his sister's tent where Zainab was waiting for him. He said:

"I heard her [Lady Zainab (s)] say to the Imam 'Have you tested your companions, for I fear that they will abandon you in your hour of need?' The Imam replied 'By Allah! I have tried their loyalties. They are all as eager to die for me as a baby is for the bosom of its mother'."

"When I heard this conversation with Zainab, I wept. Then I went and told Habib Ibn Muzahir about it. Habib said 'By Allah! If it would not be pre-empting the order of the Imam, I would attack the enemy at this very moment'. I said 'I feel it is the women within the tents that are causing such anxiety and concern to Lady Zainab, it is appropriate that we gather the men and console her by speaking of our loyalty to her brother'."

"Habib Ibn Muzahir gathered the men and explained the situation to them. They were all eager to show their willingness to engage in combat and demonstrate their unshakable resolve to die for Imam Hussain. Habib prayed for all of them. Then we all went to the tent of the women and called out: 'Oh women of the household of the Messenger of Allah! These are the swords of your defenders that have sworn not to return their swords to their sheaths without cutting off your enemies! These are their spears that they have sworn will not fall to the ground, but are to be driven into the hearts of your adversaries!' At this the women, weeping and wailing, came rushing out of the tents saying 'Oh pure soldiers! Defend the honour of the daughters and the women of the household of the Messenger of Allah and the Commander of the faithful.' We all wept and consoled them"[2].

1 al-Tabarsi, *I'ilaam al-Wara*, page 28. For a full commentary on this saying, see the following chapter of this book.

2 al-Muqarram, *Maqtal al-Husain*. Quoted in Ishtihardi, Mohammed,

These narrations portray the concern that Imam Hussain (a) and his companions had for the women of the Ahlul Bayt (a). They were aware that after their martyrdom, the women would not have any help or protection, save Allah (swt). They consoled Lady Umm Kulthum (s) and Lady Zainab (s) for they would have to find the strength to care for the widows and the orphans.

The Day of Ashura

It is widely accepted that the entire army of Imam Hussain (a) consisted of little more than one hundred members[1] whilst the army of Yazid are narrated to have numbered up to one hundred thousand men[2].

On the 10th of Muharram, the day of Ashura, Imam Hussain (a) watched each of his companions and close family ride out to the battlefield and never return. When he saw that a large number of them had died, he took hold of his sacred beard and said *"Allah's wrath intensified against the Jews for having attributed a son to Him, and His Wrath intensified against the Christians who made Him one of three, and His Wrath also intensified against the Zoroastrians who worshipped the sun and the moon instead of worshipping Him. And His Wrath intensified against people who collectively agreed to kill the son of their Prophet's daughter. By Allah! I shall never agree with them about anything they want me to do till I meet Allah drenched in my blood".* Then he called out: *"Is there anyone who would defend the ladies of the Messenger of Allah?!".* Hearing him, the women cried and wailed[3].

Lamentations II pages 44-45

1   Munfared, Ali Nazari, *Imam Hussain and the Tragic Saga of Kerbala*, page 188

2   al-Muqarram, *Maqtal al-Husain*, page 160

3   Ibn Tawus, *Al-Luhuf*, page 57

When Abul Fadhl al-Abbas (a) was killed, Imam Hussain (a) turned to see that no one was there to help him against his enemies. He saw his family members and companions lying slaughtered on the ground; he heard the wailing of the orphans and the cries of the widows. As loud as he could, he called out *"Is there anyone who defends the sanctity of the Messenger of Allah? Is there anyone who believes in the Unity of Allah and who fears Allah in our regard? Is there anyone who comes to our rescue and who wishes by doing so to please Allah?"*. The women's voices grew even louder as they cried[1].

Before his final combat with the enemy, the Imam (a) came to Lady Umm Kulthum (s) and said *"Oh sister! Take great care of my suckling child Ali Asghar, for he is only six months old"*. Lady Umm Kulthum (s) replied *"Oh brother! Your child has not tasted water for three days. Go to the people and ask for some water for him"*. The Imam (a) took Ali Asghar to his chest and advanced towards the enemy. He stood in front of the enemy exposing Ali Asghar to them and said *"Oh people! What has this child done to you? If you have any enmity, then it is with me. You have killed my sons, my brothers, and my companions. This child cannot fight you. Come and quench his thirst. Do you not see how he burns with thirst and is about to give his life?"*. The Imam (a) had not even finished speaking when on the order of Umar Ibn Sa'ad, Hurmalah made the thirsty throat of Ali Asghar the target of his three pronged arrow[2].

With Imam Hussain (a) all alone, his son Imam Zain al-Abideen (a) stood up. He was leaning on a staff and dragging a sword. He was sick and could hardly move, Imam Hussain (a) called on his sister Lady Umm Kulthum

1 Ibid, page 65

2 Ha'iri, Mohammed Mahdi, *Ma'ali al-Sibtayn*. Quoted in: Ishtihardi, Mohammed, *Lamentations II*, page 79

(s) saying *"Confine him so that the world may not run out of the progeny of Muhammad"*, so she took him back to his bed. Imam Hussain (a) embraced and comforted him saying *"Oh son, you are the purest and the noblest of my descent. You are the guardian in my place of these destitute and oppressed orphans and widows. They have no one except you to save them from their enemies. Be kind to them and a source of comfort for them"*. Then he called out, *"Oh Zainab! Oh Umm Kulthum! Oh Sakinah! Oh Ruqayyah! Oh Fatimah! Hear my words and understand that this son of mine will assume my position. He is the Imam whose obedience is obligatory"*[1].

The Martyrdom of Imam Hussain (a)

As Imam Hussain (a) resolved to engage in his final battle with the enemies, he called out: *"Oh Sakinah, Oh Fatima, Oh Zainab, Oh Umm Kulthum peace be with you from me. This is the final congregation. Your time of great tribulation and sorrow has approached"*. The Imam (a) wept as he offered them peace. *"May the merciful Lord not make you weep! Why do you shed tears my brother?"* asked Lady Zainab (s). *"How should I not cry when in a little while you will be driven between the enemies?"* replied the tearful Imam (a). The wails and cries arose from the women as they heard the Imam (a) say *"Farewell! Farewell! Separation! Separation!"*[2].

After the Martyrdom of Imam Hussain

When the Imam (a) fell to the ground, Dhul Janah, his horse, began to circle around him warding off the enemy's

---

1 For a full commentary of this narration, see the following chapter of this book

2 *Ma'ali al-Sibtayn*. Quoted in: Ishtihardi, Mohammed, *Lamentations II*, pages 82-85

attack from the Imam (a). When the horse was left alone it went to the blood soaked body of Imam Hussain (a) and placed its forelock upon him until it was coloured with his blood. Then the horse turned to the tents, galloping towards them neighing in a way that filled the air. Lady Zainab (s) hearing the neighing of the horse turned to Lady Umm Kulthum (s) and said *"This is the horse of our brother Hussain coming to the tents. It may have brought some water"*. Lady Umm Kulthum (s) rushed out of the tent and saw the horse without its mount. She beat her hands on her head and tore apart her veil and cried out: *"By Allah, Hussain has been killed!"* Lady Zainab (s) began to cry and lament the Imam (a) as she heard the cries of Lady Umm Kulthum (s)[1].

One narration states that when Lady Umm Kulthum (s) heard the neighing of Dhul Janah, she ran out to greet the horse. When she saw it was without a rider or companion she began to weep and recited the following lines of poetry:

"My calamity is so great
I cannot even explain it through poetry,
I cannot begin to comprehend it
through my knowledge and thoughts,
You approached the event and it has shocked me,
I used to honour every neighbour
but today, look at him, laid down on the earth.

If it was not for my patience
which encompasses my every thought,
It is as if on every side of his body
there is a person matching my thoughts.
I had hoped for many beautiful things,

1 Ibid pages 94-95

had it not been for this destiny which happened to him,
Now al-Jawad has returned,
there is no welcome for his arrival except for seeking revenge
for the sake of Hussain.
It is not the fault of al-Jawad
that Allah has made him miss his horse,
But he has also protected him from harm.
Oh my soul! Be patient in this world and its trials
This is Hussain going to the Lord of the Heavens"

When the other ladies heard the poem, they came out of the tents and saw the blood soaked horse; they began to slap their cheeks and tear at their dresses shouting: *"Oh Muhammad! Oh Ali! Oh Hassan! Oh Hussain! Today Muhammad al-Mustafa has died! Today Ali al-Murtadha has died! Today Fatima az-Zahra has died!"*.

Then Lady Umm Kulthum (s) leaned toward her sister, Lady Zainab (s), and said: *"Time has caused us to bear this calamity and torn into us with its teeth and claws! Time has sent us to a strange land and it has forced us to that which we were afraid of. And time has surprised us about our own relations. And with its two hands it has separated our strength. And it caused my brother to enter into tragedy. The calamity has blinded and engulfed us. Hussain, the land has become glittering and how he became a shining glory! What has befallen me, if only the smallest of it was to befall on something else, it would complain to all of existence! It is so sorrowful for me to have to leave without the personality of Hussain and to find him buried under the earth. Nothing has remained for me to seek protection with, if time has defeated me. The hands of time have torn us while our grandfather, the Messenger of Allah, the glorious uncle, had the very best of conduct"*[1].

---

1 Abu Mikhnaf, *Maqtal*, page 150. Quoted in: Shirazi, H., *Mawsu'atu Kamila (Kalimat as-Sayeda Zainab)*, page 49-50

Another tradition states that when Dhul Janah came back towards the tents of the caravan, Lady Umm Kulthum (s) beat her head with her hands and repeatedly cried *"Oh Mohammad!"*[1].

It is also narrated that Lady Umm Kulthum (s) cried out: *"Oh Muhammad! Oh father! Oh Ali ! Oh Ja'far! Oh Hamzah! Here is Husain in the open plain in Kerbala!"*[2]. *"His head has been cut from his neck! His turban and robes have been taken from him!".* Then she fell unconscious from the grief[3].

When Imam Hussain (a) was killed, people began to loot his belongings and anything they could find in his tents. They then set the tents ablaze. People raced to rob the ladies of the Ahlul Bayt (a). The daughters of Lady Fatima (s) tearfully ran away with their hair uncovered[4]. Headscarves were snatched, rings were pulled from their fingers, earrings were taken out, and so were ankle rings[5]. A man attacked Lady Umm Kulthum (s) and snatched her earrings in such a way that her earlobes were torn and bleeding[6].

Fatima as-Sughra, the young daughter of Imam Hussain (a) narrates: *"I was standing at the side of a tent and lamenting over the mutilated bodies of my father and his faithful companions. I saw horsemen galloping over their bod-*

1 al-Majlisi, *Jila ul-Ayoon*, page 207

2 al-Majlisi, *Bihar al-Anwar*, vol. 10, page 206; see also al-Khawarizmi, M., *Maqtal al-Hussain*, vol. 2 page 37

3 Bahrani, Hashim, *Awalim Syedatin Nisaa*, vol.2, hadith number 1015

4 There is a difference of opinion amongst scholars about whether the ladies were without *any* hair covering, or whether it was only their *face* covering that was taken.

5 Ibn Athir, *al-Kamil fi Tareekh*, vol. 4 page 32; see also at-Tabari, *Tareekh at-Tabari*, vol. 6, page 260

6 Shubbar, Mohammad Jawad, *Al-Dam'a al-Sakiba*, page 348; see also Sadooq, *Amaali*, section 31, hadith number 2; and al-Majlisi, *Bihar al-Anwar*. Quoted in: Ishtihardi, M., *Lamentations III*, page 2.

ies and advancing toward us. I was filled with fear and began to wonder whether they would kill us or take us as captives. A man among them rode to the women and began to stab them with the end of his spear, removing and looting their veils and outer coverings. The women cried out in desperation as they tried to flee their attacker. I trembled with fear and hid behind my aunt, Umm Kulthum, for protection. At this moment I saw an enemy running towards me. I too ran and thinking that I had escaped from him, he struck at my back with the knot of his spear; I fell onto my face. He pulled at my earrings tearing my ears and he took away my face covering. The dripping blood from my ears covered my face and head and I lost consciousness.[1] *When I regained consciousness I saw my aunt Umm Kulthum sitting beside me weeping"*[2].

Lady Zainab (s) gathered the women and the children, she realised that two young children could not be found. She called out to Lady Umm Kulthum (s), and went to look for the children. After a long search in the plains of the desert they found the two children resting underneath a thorn bush in each other's embrace. Nothing could have prepared the two sisters to bear the tragic deaths of these two infants who had died from fear and hunger as they tried to wake them. Only Allah (swt) knows what prevailed over their hearts at that moment[3]. Lady Umm Kulthum (s) *"spent the night busy in gathering the children and taking away the fear from them"*[4].

---

2 al-Majlisi, *Bihar al-Anwar*. Quoted in: Ishtihardi, Mohammed, *Lamentations III*, page 4

3 al-Muqarram, *Maqtal al-Husain*, page 300; see also al-Qazwini, *Ta'allum al-Zahra*, page 130

1 al-Ha'iri, Hassan Ibn Ali al-Yazdi *Anwar al-Shahadah*. Quoted in: Ishtihardi, Mohammed, *Lamentations III*, page 12

4 Zumaizan, Saeed Rasheed, *Nisaa al-Hawl al-Hussain*, page 52

AFTER ASHURA

On the day after the battle, just after high noon, Umar Ibn Sa'ad left the land of Kerbala for Kufa with the women, children, the bondmaids and the surviving families of Imam Hussain's (a) companions[1]. They mounted camels without saddles; this was how the Turks and Romans treated prisoners of war. Lady Umm Kulthum, Zainab as-Sughra (s) was amongst them[2]. It is narrated that Lady Umm Kulthum (s) asked: *"How can they take us on top of the camel while we are the flowers of the Messenger? Tell them to stay away and we will place one another on the camels!"*. Lady Zainab (s) then came with Lady Umm Kulthum (s) and called the women one by one and lifted them up to the camels until no one remained except Lady Zainab (s). She looked right and left and saw Imam Zain al-Abideen (a) and called to him: *"Stand up, Oh son of my brother and climb (the camel)"*. The Imam (a) replied *"Oh my aunt! You climb and leave me with them."*

The ladies pleaded: *"For the love of Allah! Please take us to those killed"*. When they saw how their loved ones had lost their limbs and trampled bodies were severed by arrows and spears, they screamed and beat their faces in anguish[3].

When Lady Umm Kulthum (s) saw the mutilated body of her brother, she called out to her grandfather: *"Oh Apostle of Allah! Come and see how the body of your son is discarded upon the plains without even the ceremonial washing! The blowing sands have placed a shroud upon him while the flowing blood from his jugular veins has washed him! Oh Messenger! See how your daughters are humiliated and taken as captives while the*

1 al-Qummi, Abbas, *Nafas al-Mahmoom*, page 204

2 Mamqani, *Tanqeeh*. Quoted in: Munfared, Ali Nazari, *Imam Hussain and the Tragic Saga of Kerbala*, pages 305-306

3 al-Khawarizmi, M., *Maqtal al-Hussain*, vol. 2 page 39

*heads of the shining moons are raised on the ends of spears!
There is no advocate protecting them and the heads of his children are raised upon spears shining like the moons!"*[1].

Lady Umm Kulthum's (s) tears continued to flow. She remained by her brother taking in his fragrance; she pulled
his body close to her and then called out *"Oh grandfather!
Where are you now? Bring my brother to be with me!*[2]*"*.

The Captives Taken to Kufa

Abdullah Ibn Abbas (a) narrates that Lady Umm Kulthum
(s) called one of the captors: *"Woe unto you! With this one
thousand dirhams, keep the head of Hussain on top of the
camel and behind us so that the people should be busy watching the head of Hussain instead of us".* The captor took the
money and followed her instruction, but the next day
when he went to look at the money it had all changed into
stones. One side read *"And do not think that Allah is heed-
less of what the unjust do. He only respites them to a day on
which the eyes shall be fixed open"* (14:42), and on the other
*"And they who act unjustly shall know to what final place of
turning they shall return to"* (26:227)[3].

When the daughters of the Commander of the Faithful
(a) entered Kufa, the city's residents gathered to see them.
Lady Umm Kulthum (s) exclaimed: *"Oh people of Kufa! Do
you not have any sense of shame before Allah and His Messenger so you look at the ladies of the Prophet (s)?*[4]*".*

---

1 al-Birjandi, Mohammed Baqir, *Kibrit al-Ahmar*. Quoted in:
Ishtihardi, Mohammed, *Lamentations III*, page 14

2 al-Kaashi, Abd al-Wahhab, *at-Tareeq ila Mambr al-Hussain*, vol. 8,
page 387

3 al-Majlisi, *Bihar al-Anwar*, vol. 45, page 304

4 Shubbar, Mohammad Jawad, *Al-Dam'a al-Sakiba*, page 364. For a
full commentary of this narration, see the following chapter

A reporter narrated: *"I was returning to Kufa after performing the Hajj. Celebrations were taking place in the city and the governor had declared that day an official public holiday. Upon enquiring I was told that the members of the family of an outlaw were being brought to Kufa from Kerbala. The palace was surrounded by soldiers and the sounds of beating drums and trumpets could be heard from all directions. My sight fell on the severed head of Imam Hussain, raised on the end of a spear and I saw Imam Sajjad tied to an unsaddled camel. After this I saw women being brought as captives. From amongst them one was shouting to an on-looking crowd. I asked someone who the woman was and I was told that it was Lady Umm Kulthum, the daughter of Ali Ibn Abi Talib".*

He continued saying that *"the captives were stationed in front of the door of Banu Khazimah. At this moment Lady Umm Kulthum's glance fell on the head of her brother, Imam Hussain. In despair she tore her outer garments as she recited the following verses:*

What will you answer if the Prophet were to ask you?
What have you done while you were the last of nations
To my progeny and household after my death?

From them are captives and others covered with their blood
This was not the recompense to which I directed you
That after me you deal with my kin with such evil
Indeed I fear that a curse will come upon you
Like the chastisement befalling the previous nations"[1]

The governor of Kufa, Ibn Ziyad, was not affected by this incident. He ordered the captives to be brought to him. The ladies of the Messenger of Allah (swt) arrived in the

1 al-Birjandi, Mohammed Baqir, *Ma'ali al-Sibtayn*. Quoted in: Ishtihardi, Mohammed, *Lamentations III*, page 24

most wretched condition. Ibn Ziyad imprisoned the captives. A stone with a letter fastened to it was thrown into the jail and it read: *"A messenger has been sent to Damascus to Yazid to narrate your story to him. He will arrive back in Kufa at such and such a time. Know that if you hear chants of takbir* [the cry Allah (swt) is the Greatest] *he has ordered your killing otherwise you will be safe".* Upon the return of the messenger no *takbir* was heard but Yazid had ordered the captives be taken to him[1].

THE CAPTIVES TAKEN TO DAMASCUS

Imam Muhammad al-Baqir (a) narrates *"I asked my father Ali Ibn Hussain how he was moved from Kufa to Damascus[2]. He stated 'they rode me on an unsaddled camel, they put my father's head on a spear and the women behind us on unsaddled mules, while followed by spear holders who hit any one of us who were weeping! This lasted until we entered Damascus'[3].*

The group were taken through at least eighteen different towns and cities[4]. When the captives reached the city of Ba'albak, the governor sent the public to meet them. They celebrated carrying flags and bringing their children to see the captives. To this, Lady Umm Kulthum (s) said *"May Allah destroy their developments, not freshen their water and curtail the force of the tyrants!"*[5].

---

2 at-Tabari, *Tareekh at-Tabari*, vol. 5, page 234

3 It is agreed upon by all historians that Imam al-Baqir (a) was present throughout the event of Kerbala and therefore his question is not due to his absence, rather it is either due to his desire to bring to mind the oppression his father faced, or to teach those present of those incidents

4 al-Majlisi, *Bihar al-Anwar*, vol. 45, page 145

5 Munfared, Ali Nazari, *Imam Hussain and the Tragic Saga of Kerbala*, pages 353-363

5 al-Majlisi, *Bihar al-Anwar*, vol. 126, page 45

THE EVENTS IN DAMASCUS

As the caravan was nearing the city of Damascus, Lady Umm Kulthum (s) approached Shimr Ibn Dhil Jawshan, the commander in chief of the army detaining them, and said *"I wish to request something of you. First, enter into the city from the gate that has the least spectators. Second tell your men to carry the spears bearing our men away from us so that the onlookers may look at them and be distracted from looking at us"*. Shimr acted in direct opposition to these requests and brought the captives through the main gate keeping the holy heads with them[1].

Sahl Ibn Sa'ad al-Sa'edi the companion of the Holy Prophet (s) narrates *"I saw a beautiful light emanating from the spear; it was from the head of Abul Fadhl al-Abbas. Then I saw a horseman who had a spear in his hand with Imam Hussain's head on it! I also saw Lady Umm Kulthum trying to cover herself with a very old veil"*[2].

Imam Zain al-Abideen (a) narrates *"In Damascus we were subjected to the worst of treatment. We were subjected to seven humiliating and agonising difficulties that were unprecedented in the course of the whole of our captivity.*

First, we were made to stand in the market place surrounded by crowds beating drums and blowing trumpets of victory. The soldiers circled around us and were poking at us with their spears and swords.

Second, the heads of the martyrs were placed between the camels carrying the women. The heads of my father and Uncle Abbas were kept in front of my aunts Zainab and Umm Kulthum whilst the heads of my brother Ali Akbar and cousin Qasim were kept in front of my sisters Sakinah and Fatima.

---

1   Ibn Tawus, *Al-Luhuf*, page 99

2   al-Zakhkhar, *Qamqaame*, page 556. Quoted in: Munfared, A. *The Tragic Saga of Kerbala*, page 369

The soldiers would mock and play with the heads and at times the heads would fall from the top of the spears and come beneath the hooves of the horses and camels.

Third, the women of Damascus would throw boiling water and burning firewood on our heads from the top of the roofs of their homes. My hands were tied to my neck and I could not remove the burning wood from my head. The fire burnt both the turban I was wearing and the skin of my head.

Fourth, from sunrise until dusk they paraded us in crowded streets and squares amidst mocking crowds clapping with joy and dancing at our loss, as the commanders shouted: 'Oh people, kill these captives! They have no sanctity in Islam!'.

Fifth, we were tied with a single rope and were dragged through the alleys where the Christians and the Jews resided. The soldiers called out 'These are the sons and daughters of those men who killed your fathers at Khaybar and Khandaq! This is the day to avenge your loss from them'. Each one of the Jews and Christians threw sand, stones and sticks at us!

Sixth, we were taken to the slave market to be sold off as slaves but Allah saved us from this horrific fate.

Seventh, we were detained in a place without a roof. There was no protection from the heat of the day or the cold of the night! We were starved of food and lived in constant fear of being savaged by the wild beasts"[1].

Lady Fatima as-Sughra (s), the daughter of Imam Hussain (a), narrates: *"Yazid placed us where the sun shone directly onto our skins to such an extent that our skins burnt and peeled off"*[2].

Hind, the wife of Yazid, had stayed in the house of Imam Ali (a) after the death of her father until Mu'awiya

---

1 Ali, Hakim Amanat, *Tadhkirat al-Shuhada*. Quoted in: Ishtihardi, Mohammed, *Lamentations III*, pages 57-58

2 Sadooq, *al-Amaali*, section 31, hadith number 4

married her to his son. She was in Damascus and was not aware of the events in Kerbala. On the day when the captives entered the city she was informed of the parade and donned her finest dress and sat to observe the prisoners. Lady Zainab (s) saw Hind and turned to Lady Umm Kulthum (s) and asked *"do you recognise this woman?"*. She replied to the negative. Lady Zainab (s) said *"this woman is none other than our maid Hind, the daughter of Abdallah"*. Lady Umm Kulthum (s) fell silent and lowered her head; Lady Zainab (s) did the same.

Hind came forward, stood on her chair, faced Lady Zainab (a) and said *"Oh sister, why do you not lift your head?"*. Lady Zainab (s) did not reply. Hind asked *"what city are you from?"* to which was the response *"from the city of Medina"*. Hearing the name of Medina, Hind stood down from her chair and said *"the best of greetings be with the people of Medina"*.

Lady Zainab (s) asked *"why did you step down from your chair?"* and Hind replied *"I show this respect in reverence to the people of Medina. I would like to ask you about a family residing in Medina"*. Lady Zainab (s) stated *"ask whatever you desire"*. Hind, with tears in her eyes said *"I want to ask you about the family of Ali; I was their maid for some time"*.

Lady Zainab (s) replied *"Who from the family of Ali do you ask of?"* and Hind responded *"I want to know about Hussain, his brothers, his children and the rest of the children of Ali; I want to know about my Lady Zainab, her sister Lady Umm Kulthum and all the women of the families of Lady Fatima"*.

At this, Lady Zainab (s) began to weep and with a sorrowful voice said *"Oh Hind! If you ask about the house of Ali, then know, that we have abandoned it in Medina and we wait to take the news of the death of his family back to the people of Medina. But if it is Hussain you ask of, then that is his severed head on the end of the spear. If you ask about Abbas and the rest of Ali's children we have left them behind in the deserts of Kerbala, their bodies dismembered and heads severed from their shoulders like sacrificial sheep! If it is Zain al-Abideen you ask of, there he is, unable to move due to severity of illness and pains. If you ask of Zainab then know that I am Zainab the daughter of Ali and this is Umm Kulthum and those women you see as prisoners are the rest of the women related to Lady Fatima the most pure".*

Hearing the words of Lady Zainab and realising what had taken place, Hind let out a cry and wailed *"Alas my Imam! Oh my Master! Oh my Hussain, I wish I would have been blind and not seen the daughters of Lady Fatima the radiant, in this state!"*[1].

Before they were brought to Yazid's court, they were tied with ropes. The beginning of the rope was around the neck of Imam Zain al-Abideen (a), then around the necks of Lady Zainab (s), Lady Umm Kulthum (s) and all the daughters of the Messenger of Allah (swt). Whenever they walked too slowly, they were whipped. This continued until they were brought to Yazid, who was then sitting on his throne. Imam Zain al-Abideen (a) asked him *"What do you think the reaction of the Messenger of Allah might have been had he seen us looking like this?"*. Everyone wept and Yazid ordered the ropes to be cut off[2].

After the famous sermons of Lady Zainab (s) and Imam Zain al-Abideen (a) there became unrest and pressure toward Yazid for his crimes against the Ahlul Bayt (a). Imam Zain al-Abideen (a) secured their release and began the journey back to Medina. When departing, Yazid gave

1 Ishtihardi, Mohammed, *Lamentations III*, pages 75-76

2 Ibn Athir, *al-Kamil fi Tareekh*, vol. 4 page 35; see also al-Yaf'i, A., *Mir'at al-Jinan*, page 341

the caravan a great deal of wealth and told Lady Umm Kulthum (s): *"These are compensations for the tragedy you have faced."* She replied *"How insolent and shameless you are! You slaughtered my brother Hussain and this house and give us wealth instead?! We shall never accept this property!"*[1].

FROM DAMASCUS TO KERBALA

The caravan continued their journey until they reached a road which forked, one path led toward Medina and the other back to Kerbala. The caravan returned to Kerbala to bury the heads of their beloved family members on the 20th Safar 61 AH[2].

Upon entering the plains, Lady Umm Kulthum (s) beat her face and cried out: *"Today Muhammad the chosen, Ali the inspired and Fatima the radiant, have passed away!"* To this the other women beat their faces and wailed[3].

THE AHLUL BAYT RETURN TO MEDINA

The family of the Prophet (s) departed Kerbala again but this time to return to their home-city of Medina. As they approached the city Lady Umm Kulthum (s) became overwhelmed and spoke out saying:

> *"Oh city of our Grandfather! Accept us not*
> *For with sighs and griefs we come;*
> *We left you surrounded by kith and kin*
> *And returned with neither sons nor men"*[4]

---

1   al-Majlisi, *Bihar al-Anwar*, vol. 45, page 197

2   al-Majlisi, *Bihar al-Anwar*, vol. 65, page 130

3   Ibid, vol. 65, page 130

4   For the complete lamentation and commentary, see the following chapter of this book

Then she took both knobs of the mosque's door and cried out: *"Oh grandfather! I mourn to you about my brother al-Hussain!"*[1].

Conclusion

Lady Umm Kulthum (s) did not only witness the event that changed the landscape of Islam, but her role as a supportive sister, a guardian of orphans and a narrator of the tragedies that befell her family, were integral to the continuation of Imam Hussain's (a) revolution. After their return to Medina, the ladies who grew up in the lap of Prophethood held mourning ceremonies for the Master of Martyrs, Imam al-Hussain (a). They put on coarse clothes, they shrouded themselves in black, and they continued to weep and wail day and night[2]. Through these mourning ceremonies, Lady Umm Kulthum (s) and the ladies of the household of the Prophet (s), narrated the events in Kerbala, Kufa and Damascus, and spread the true Prophetic message of Islam.

In the following chapter some of these narrations have been quoted in full alongside a detailed commentary.

---

1 al-Majlisi, *Bihar al-Anwar*, vol. 45, page 197; see also al-Qazwini, *Riyaa al-Azan*, page 163. Quoted in: Muqarram, *Maqtal*, chapter 71, narration 1095

2 al-Muqarram, *Maqtal al-Husain*, chapter 71, hadith number 5

Lady Umm Kulthum's Key Contributions in Kerbala, Kufa and Medina

Shaping History

The following key contributions, each of which have a detailed commentary, demonstrate that Lady Umm Kulthum (s) had a pivotal role in shaping the history of Islam and the spread of the message of Imam Hussain (a). The first narration portrays the conversation between Lady Umm Kulthum (s) and Imam Hussain (a) on the eve of Ashura. The second narration is recorded on the day of Ashura; when Imam Hussain (a) was all alone, it was Lady Umm Kulthum (s) that he called upon to preserve Imamate. The third is an illuminating description of Lady Umm Kulthum's (s) character. The next narration describes how she preserved the dignity of the Ahlul Bayt (a) on the streets of Kufa. The fifth is her sermon on the streets of Kufa, and the last is her emotional and poetic lamentation at the gates of the city of her grandfather.

Narration 1: Advice of Imam Hussain to Lady Umm Kulthum on the Eve of Ashura

وجعلت أمّ كلثوم تنادي:

وا أحمداه ، وا عليّاه ، وا أمّاه ، وا أخاه ، واحسيناه ، واضيعتنا بعدك يا ابا عبدالله .

فعزّاها الحسين عليه السلام وقال لها : يا أختاه ، تعزّي بعزاء الله ، فإنّ سكان السماوات يفنون ، وأهل الأرض كلّهم يموتون وجميع البريّة يهلكون.

ثمّ قال : يا أختاه ، يا أمّ كلثوم ، وأنت يازينب ، وأنت يا فاطمة ، وأنت يا رباب ، انظرن إذا أنا قتلت فلا تشققنّ عليّ جيبا ، ولا تخمشنّ عليّ وجهاً ، ولا تقلن هجراً .

It is narrated, that on the plains of Kerbala, Lady Umm Kulthum (s) called out: *"Oh Ahmad! Oh Ali! Oh Mother! Oh Brother! Oh Hussain! Oh how much we are to lose after you, Oh father of Abdullah!"*

Imam Hussain (a) consoled her *"Oh my sister, be consoled by the consolation of Allah. For surely those who live in the heavens, they will perish; and all those who live in the earth will die; and all the creatures will be destroyed".*

Then he said *"Oh my sister! Oh Umm Kulthum! And you Zainab, and you Fatima and you Rubab! Watch, if I am killed, do not tear your dresses and do not beat your faces and do not be overcome with grief*"[1].

COMMENTARY

This narration provides an insight into the relationship between Lady Umm Kulthum (s) and Imam Hussain (a). Just as her father Imam Ali (a) chose to spend his final hours in the company of his beloved daughter, Imam Hussain (a) spent time on the eve of Ashura consoling his sister and advising her. This shows the high level of regard the Imams (a) had for Lady Umm Kulthum (s).

Lady Umm Kulthum (s) called out: "Wā Aḥmadāh, Wā 'Aliyyāh!". In Arabic, this is a call of distress, in a time of extreme grief when urgent assistance is needed. In regular conversation, if a person is addressed or summoned, the word Yā is used, for example: Yā 'Alī. The word Wā instead of Yā has been used in times of distress by the Ahlul Bayt (a). For example after the death of the Holy Prophet (s), those who oppressed the Ahlul Bayt (a) demanded that homage be paid to the rulers of the time. Imam Ali (a) refused. They attacked the house and it is narrated that *"they took Ali by force and with harshness from the house to the mosque so that he should pay allegiance. Salmaan* [al-Farsi] *was watching the incident and exclaimed: 'How can they do this, to this* [kind of] *person, for that* [the divine role of leadership]*? I swear by Allah, if Ali had taken an oath with Allah the heavens would have collapsed upon the earth!'"*. The narrator continues that *"they gathered around him* [Imam Ali (a)] *and were pushing him though he did not accept it; he called out 'Waa Hamzah! But I do not have Hamzah today!*

1 Bahrani, Hashim, *Awalim Syeda an-Nisaa*, vol. 2, page 1014. Quoted in: Shirazi, H., *Mawsu'atu Kamila (Kalimat Syeda Zainab)*, page 47

Waa Ja'fara! But I do not have Ja'far today! Oh my Lord! I am well pleased with your destiny and so patient with the trials'"[1].

The source of Lady Umm Kulthum's (s) distress was the realisation that there would be no loss like the loss of her brother; she said *"Oh how much we are to lose after you, Oh father of Abdullah!"*. Imam Hussain (a) was the last member of *Ahlul Kisaa*[2], the last infallible to have witnessed the period of revelation, and the last son of the daughter of the Prophet (s).

Upon hearing these lamentations from his sister, Imam Hussain (a) offered some relief by reminding her of the fate of every person and everything in existence. As Lady Umm Kulthum (s) was overcome with the anguish of envisaging life without her dear brother, the Imam (a) resorts to a rational appeal. The statement *"be consoled by the consolation of Allah"* is an intriguing declaration by Imam Hussain (a). This is because it appears to be an entirely unique statement from a member of Ahlul Bayt (a); even when the Prophet (s) narrated the incident of Kerbala to Lady Fatima (s) or his wives he did not use these particular words.

Imam Hussain (a) did not ask his sister to take comfort from anyone else but Allah (swt). While it would have been customary for the Imams (a) to advise people to be God-conscious and to rely on Allah (swt), there seems to be a special meaning in the advice to Lady Umm Kulthum (s). The "consolation of Allah (swt)" cannot be compared to how a human comforts another through touch, sensitivity or empathy; rather it implies that Allah (swt) has a direct influence on the unfolding of events in Kerbala, as

---

1 Khafajee, *Maqatil al-Ma'sumeen*, page 107

2 These are the 'People of the Cloak' referring to the incident regarding the revelation of verse 33:33; for additional information refer to *Sahih Muslim*, book 31, hadith 5955

explained in the verse *"Blessed is He whose hand is (over) the kingdom"* (67:1). There are four ways to understand the concept of the "consolation of Allah (swt)".

The first is that the event of Kerbala had been pre-ordained by Allah (swt) as part of His divine plan. The Prophet (s) has mentioned the event of Kerbala and the fate of Imam Hussain (a) to the people many times when Imam Hussain (a) was just a child. Abdullah Ibn Abbas (a) is narrated to have said *"We and the Ahlul Bayt did not doubt that al-Hussain Ibn Ali would be killed in al-Taff* [Kerbala]"[1].One interpretation therefore, is that Imam Hussain (a) wanted to remind Lady Umm Kulthum (s) that no one can change what Allah (swt) has decreed. He said *"if the sand-grouse is left, it will rest in its place"*[2] meaning that the enemies would never spare him.

The second interpretation is that the Imam (a) was reminding his sister that to be "consoled by Allah (swt)" was the reward of seeking the highest pleasure of Allah (swt). That the event of Kerbala was not ordinary in the eyes of Allah (swt) and every moment of physical and emotional adversity would be rewarded. The Holy Qur'an states: *"And give glad tidings to the patient, who when a tribulation befalls them, they say 'Indeed unto Allah do we belong and unto Him shall we return.' Those are they on whom are blessings and mercy from their Lord"* (2:155-157). It is also narrated that Imam as-Sadiq (a) asked: *"Have you not heard the words of Allah the Exalted in this verse: 'Oh tranquil soul at complete ease! Return to your Lord, well pleased with Him and His being well pleased with you'* (89:27-30). *Here Imam Hussain is referred to as Allah being well pleased with him"*[3].

1 Nisapuri, H., *Al-Mustadrak al-Sahihain*, vol.3, page 179

2 al-Qummi, Abbas, *Nafas al-Mahmoom*, chapter 20, section 25; see also Ishtihardi, Mohammad, *Lamentations II*, page 77

3 al-Qummi, Abbas, *Nafas al-Mahmoom*, chapter 2, Hadith 21

The 'consolation of Allah (swt)' may also refer to Imam al-Mahdi (may Allah (swt) hasten his reappearance), who will take revenge for the oppression and suffering of the Ahlul Bayt (a). This was something frequently emphasised by the Imam (a) throughout the journey. On the eve of Ashura, Imam Hussain (a) said to his companion: *"By Allah! Receive the glad tidings of paradise. By Allah! After we have been killed, a time will elapse after which we will be raised once again. That will be the time of the coming of al-Qa'im from among us. He will take revenge on our enemies and we will witness the chastisement being given to them"*[1].

The final understanding of this advice is taken from the context of the complete statement. This is a likely interpretation as the Imam (a) uses a continuous tense, indicated by the Arabic words fa inna. He said: *"Oh my sister, be consoled by the consolation of Allah. For surely those who live in the heavens, they will perish; and all those who live in the earth will die; and all the creatures with be destroyed"*. Here, the 'consolation of Allah (swt)' is spoken about in the context of three groups of people. The first group are those who reside in the heavens. They are described as yafnūn which is derived from the word fānin as the Holy Qur'an states *"All that is on it must perish; but the face of your Lord will remain forever"* (55:26-27). The second group are the people of the earth who will die. This differentiates the first group, as the residents of the heavens do not possess a soul, whilst their human counterparts on the earth do. The last group are the rest of the creatures who will not experience either of these conditions. Imam Hussain (a) says they will meet yahlikū 'the destroyed', derived from halaka as in the verse *"and when we wish to destroy a population, we send a definite order to those among them"* (17:16).

---

1 al-Muqarram, *Maqtal al-Husain* , chapter 49 entitled 'The Night Preceding Ashura'

By appealing to her understanding of these Qur'anic concepts, Imam Hussain (a) reminds his sister that those who oppress the family of the Prophet (s) will be accountable before Allah (swt). The Imam (a) tells Lady Umm Kulthum (s) to be consoled by the thought that there will be a day when "*each soul will be paid out what it has earned*" (3:25). It is with this understanding and context that the Imam (a) then addresses the other womenfolk regarding their conduct after his martyrdom. He extended this reminder: that Allah (swt) will most certainly bring about justice and therefore they should not transgress the bounds of exhibiting their grief.

This advice to Lady Umm Kulthum (s) and the ladies of Ahlul Bayt (a) often raises questions because the Imam (a) requests them to not "*beat at their faces*". Yet there are numerous traditions which record that the women of the Ahlul Bayt (a) did beat their faces after the death of Imam Hussain (a). How can these narrations be reconciled?

Firstly, emotional expression is not forbidden by the Holy Qur'an, rather it is encouraged as long as it is kept within the boundaries of law and etiquette. Two examples from the Holy Qur'an help to illustrate this point. The first is when Lady Sarah (s), the wife of Prophet Ibrahim (s), finds that she is pregnant at an old age; in reaction to this "*she struck her face and cried: A barren old woman!*"(51:29). The second is when Lady Maryam (s) gave birth to Prophet Isa (s); she was aware of the adverse reaction from her community and exclaims in distress "*Ah! Would that I had died before this and been a thing long forgotten!*" (19:23).

Secondly, narrations state that the ladies of the Ahlul Bayt (a) struck their faces and wailed in front of their Imam (a) during his lifetime. If this had not been permissible, the Imam (a) would have stated so previously. For example it is narrated that "*when the forces of Yazid planned to attack the camp of Imam Hussain, Lady Zainab came to the Imam and asked why there was so much noise [movement] outside the tents, the Imam replied that 'I just dreamt of the Holy Prophet and he said to me that I will be meeting him tomorrow.' Hearing this, Lady Zainab started crying and beating herself on the face*"[1]. Therefore, if it is permissible to perform the action during the Imam's (a) lifetime, how can it not be permissible to do so after his martyrdom?

The answer could be found in the context of the conversation. The Imam (a) states "wa lā taqulna hajrā" which is translated as *"and do not be overcome by grief"*. Whilst this translation for grief is accurate, the root of the word is from yahjuru which means to 'speak nonsense', to be 'delirious' or to engage in 'vain talk'. This was a common practise for the women of Quraysh, as they did this after the Battle of Badr. One explanation is that Imam Hussain (a) was instructing his sisters not to partake in this kind of emotional response and to always be in control of their actions. The Holy Qur'an indicates that this should be our emotional state at all times: *"you may not grieve for what has escaped you nor be exultant in what He has given to you"* (57:23).

To conclude the analysis of one of the most important conversations between Imam Hussain (a) and Lady Umm Kulthum (s), one must appreciate that the deeper value and meaning of the dialogue cannot be completely understood. On a night like the night of Ashura, a heartbroken sister spoke to her Imam (a) for one of the last times; he comforted her and advised her; through these words we can certainly appreciate her venerable position with Allah (swt) and the Imam (a).

---

1 Ibn Kathir, *al-Bidaya wan-Nihaya*, vol. 8, page 176

Narration 2: The Attempt of Imam Zain al-Abideen to Fight

روي الشيخ التستري رحمه الله استغاثات الحسين عليه السلام يوم
عاشوراء ، وعزم الإمام زين العابدين عليه السلام على الجهاد ،

فقال : فأخذ بيده عصاً يتوكّأ عليها ، وسيفاً يجرّه في الأرض
فخرج من الخيام ، وخرجت أمّ كلثوم خلفه تنادي :

يا بنيّ ، ارجع ، وهو يقول :

ياعمّتاه ، ذريني أقاتل بين يدي ابن رسول الله ، فقال الحسين
عليه السلام : يا أمّ كلثوم ، خذيه ، لئلّا تبقى الأرض خالية من
نسل آل محمد (ص) ، فأرجعته أم كلثوم.

It is narrated by Sheikh Tustari that: *"Imam al-Hussain sought help on the day of Ashura. And when Imam Zain al-Abideen was determined to go the battle, he took in his hand a staff and was leaning on it, and in the other hand took a sword dragging it along the earth and came out of the tent. Lady Umm Kulthum went out behind him and called out: 'Oh my son! Return back!'. Imam Zain al-Abideen responded 'Oh my aunt! Leave me! Leave me so I should fight in the company of the son of the Messenger of Allah!'.*

Imam al-Hussain said 'Oh Umm Kulthum! Take him back so that the earth should not remain without the offspring of Muhammad' and so she took him back in"[1].

1 Bahrani, Hashim, *Awalim Syeda an-Nisaa*, vol. 2, page 1014

COMMENTARY

This is perhaps one of the most disturbing scenes of the day of Ashura. As Imam Hussain (a) stood alone on the plains of Kerbala, he saw the mutilated bodies of his close family members and companions. He had sacrificed everything and with no one left to help, he called out: *"Is there no defender who could save the sanctity of the Messenger of Allah? Is there no believer in Allah who fears the Almighty with regard to us? Is there no helper who, for the sake of Allah may fulfil our need?"*[1]. According to narrations, this was not the first time the Imam (a) had made this call.

The call resonates on many levels. It was a call directed to the army of Yazid; if there was a person with any goodness or humanity in their heart, they had an opportunity to respond to the Imam's (a) call. As Imam Hussain (a) was the true inheritor of the Prophet (s), it was incumbent upon all of the army to respond to this plea for help, according to the Qur'anic verse: *"the Prophet has greater claim over the believers than they have over their own selves"* (33:6). The call was to any *"believer in Allah"* demonstrating that those in the army of Yazid showed their disbelief in Allah (swt) and *"turned back upon their heels"* (3:144) through their actions. The call was also to those who were not present on the plains of Kerbala. Imam Hussain (a) was calling out to the entire Muslim nation, of every generation and in every corner of the world to assist him in his mission to reform the nation of his grandfather. His sole aim was to depose not just Yazid, but *every* Yazid; every oppressor and tyrant, to spread the seeds of justice, morality and divine unity.

The Imam (a) was truly alone. Only a few weeks before he had received thousands of letters from followers ready to pay allegiance to him and promise to fight for his cause.

---

1 Qarashi, *The Life of Imam al-Hussain*, page 764

Yet on this day, there was no one to defend him or his family. It was in this situation that Imam Zain al-Abideen (a) arose from his mat with a sword in his hand, leaning on a staff, ready to fight for the son of the Prophet (s).

Imam Zain al-Abideen (a) was leaning on a staff as he was suffering from an illness which made him extremely weak. This illness was part of Allah's (swt) divine plan. However, when he heard his father's call, he was desperate to answer in any way he could, in an attempt to relieve the grandson of the Prophet (s) from the pain he was suffering.

Lady Umm Kulthum (s) was present in the tent with them, and she was aware of her nephew's illness and fragility; she would have been nursing his illness. At this point Imam Hussain (a) intervened and asked Lady Umm Kulthum (s) to take her nephew back inside the tents.

The statement the Imam (a) made is: *"take him back so that the earth should not remain without the offspring of Muhammad"*. His statement refers to the tradition: *"Unquestionably, the earth can never remain devoid of a proof of Allah over His creation"*[1], which is recorded many times by the Imams (a). Imam Hussain (a) was highlighting the importance of his son as the Imam after him. At this point, saving the life of Imam Zain al-Abideen (a) was equal to saving the religion of Islam itself. If he was killed on the battlefield on the day of Ashura, who would have given the great sermon in the court of Yazid, irrevocably destroying his lies and status and lead the spiritual and emotional revolution in remembrance of Imam Hussain (a)?

All of this was predicated by the hand of Lady Umm Kulthum (s) clasping her nephew and returning him to safety. What a contribution to Islamic history! What thanks we owe to Lady Umm Kulthum (s) for her presence and action!

1 al-Amili, Hurr, *Wasa'il as-Shi'a*, vol. 11, page 491. Quoted in: , Mutlaq, Ridha Husayni, *The Last Luminary*, page 2

Narration 3: A Description of Lady Umm Kulthum

ظلّت السيدة ام كلثوم تتحدّى اركان السلطة الامويّة من خلال

انتقادها للأعمال اللاإنسانيّة الّتي

اقترفها ضد سبايا آل البيت (عليهم السلام)

في مدينة الكوفة وفي الطريق الذي استقلّوه من كربلاء...

"Lady Umm Kulthum remained steadfast, challenging the foundations of the authority of the Umayyid family, and exposing their inhumane treatment of the family of the House (a) in the city of Kufa and on the road from Kerbala to Kufa..."[1]

Commentary

Concise and to the point; this narration is a valuable description of the virtuous qualities of Lady Umm Kulthum (s). It highlights three facets of her life from when she was led from the plains of Kerbala to her final breath in Medina.

The opening word, ẓallat, translated as "she remained steadfast" is used to describe Lady Umm Kulthum's (s) disposition during her time in captivity. An understanding of the Arabic expression uncovers the true depth of meaning of this description.

Firstly, the root of ẓallat is from the word ẓill which means shadow. Although literally, a shadow is the darkened area where light cannot reach when an object blocking it, poetically, a shadow is something that follows you in an identical manner, no matter where you go; it is a part of

1 Zumaizan, Saeed Rasheed, *Nisaa al-Hawla al-Hussain*, page 54

you that cannot be removed nor altered and mirrors exactly, the movement of the object. This phrase can be found in the Holy Qur'an in the verse: *"Have you not considered the work of your Lord, how He extends His shadow?"* (25:45).

Ẓallat is a verb which is used to describe Lady Umm Kulthum's (s) unwavering state, despite all she had seen and experienced, she had remained in 'her own state'. Her attention towards Allah (swt) did not falter; she was, in her sincerity and action during those calamities, exactly as she was at other times in her life.

This is a remarkable state to ponder over and attempt to implement in our lives. The description also sheds light on the famous tradition that Lady Zainab (s), in her enduring commitment and connection to Allah (swt) still performed her night prayer (*Salaat al-Layl*) on the night known as *Shaame Ghariba*, when the camp of Imam Hussain (a) was attacked. The narration also demonstrates how Lady Umm Kulthum (s) fulfilled the wishes of her brother, Imam Hussain (a) in his last request to remain steadfast at all times.

This state is a great lesson for all the followers of Lady Umm Kulthum (s) to try and emulate. Often when a trial presents itself, it can be a means to preclude us from remembering Allah (swt), however she showed us the virtue of remaining steadfast in times of joy and sadness.

Following this, the narration goes on to describe Lady Umm Kulthum (s) as one who was "challenging" the Ummayid family on the journey from Kerbala and in the city of Kufa. The word used is tataḥaddā which is 'to fervently and vigorously defend one's views'. One of the applicable root words is hadda, a synonym is ḥudūd which mean 'borders' or 'limits'. The term ḥudūd is also used in the Holy Qur'an in the verse: *"These are the limits as set by Allah"* (4:13) relating to the boundaries set by Allah (swt) that one cannot cross. A second root word is aḥad which means 'unique', 'indivisible' and 'the only'. Aḥad should not be confused with waḥid which is translated as the number one. Therefore, when Lady Umm Kulthum (s) was making taḥadā (her challenge) to the captors, her argument and complaint against them was undeniable; this was, of course, the killing of Imam Hussain (a) and taking women and children of the Ahlul Bayt (a) as prisoners.

The third point is that the account states her challenge was specifically toward the "foundations of the authority" of the Umayyid family. The word arkān can also be translated as pillars but in either case the word represents the base or source of something.

Although this narration speaks specifically of Lady Umm Kulthum's (s) actions in Kufa, there are other narrations which affirm her role as one who challenged the "foundations" of the Ummayid family during the period of her captivity in Damascus. It is narrated that the head of Imam Hussain (a) resembled that of his grandfather, Prophet Muhammad (s) and was shining; when she saw it raised upon the spear, she cried out: *"Oh my brother! Oh my uncle! Oh my father! Oh my grandfather! Oh my grandmother! Oh Muhammad! Oh Ali! Oh Hussain! Oh Abbas! Today the family of Muhammad has been destroyed by the hands of Abu Sufyan and Utbah (bin Rabee'ah)"*[1].

There is another lesson to be learnt here: Lady Umm Kulthum (s) did not only hold culpable those who were directly connected to the killing of Imam Hussain (a), she goes further to indicate that the blame also lies with those who planted the seeds of hatred towards the religion of Islam and the household of the Prophet (a). The Holy Qur'an alludes to this idea by telling us to *"fight the leaders of disbelief"* (9:12).

---

1 al-Kaashi, Abd al-Wahhab, *at-Tareeq ila Mambr al-Hussain*, vol. 8, page 383

These three great descriptions of Lady Umm Kulthum's
(s) steadfast nature and formidable opposition toward her
enemies resemble some of the celebrated virtues in the
Holy Qur'an. In one of the passages describing the story
of Prophet Musa (a), he is told by Allah (swt) to "*Go to the
unjust people.*" Prophet Musa (a) replies, "*They will reject
me*". Allah (swt) encourages his 'challenge' to Pharaoh's
authority by saying, "*By no means! Indeed We are with
you, hearing!*" (26:10-15). In this same way, Lady Umm
Kulthum (s) found comfort in knowing that Allah (swt) is
always with her and remained resolute in her opposition to
injustice no matter the circumstance. Her faith endured,
even after returning to the city of Medina. In fact it was the
cause of the final oppression during Lady Umm Kulthum's
(s) last days.

NARRATION 4: TAKING CHARITY IS PROHIBITED FOR US

وعند دخول السبايا مدينة الكوفة بتلك الحالة المزرية التي يحدّثنا

بها التاريخ ، كانت أمّ كلثوم تنظر إلى ذلك وقد اشتدّ بها الوجد

، وأمضّ بها المصاب ، وزاد في وجدها أن ترى أهل الكوفة

يناولون الأطفال الذين على المحامل بعض التمر والخبز والجوز ،

فصاحت بهم :

يا أهل الكوفة ، إن الصدقة علينا حرام ، وصارت تأخذ ذلك من

أيدي الأطفال وأفواههم وترمي به إلى الأرض .

قال مسلّم الجصّاص : والنّاس ، يبكون على ، ما أصابهم .

ثم إنّ أمّ كلثوم أطلعت رأسها من المحمل وقالت لهم : صه يا أهل

الكوفة ، تقتلنا رجالكم ، وتبكينا نساؤكم ! والحاكم بيننا

وبينكم الله يوم فصل القضاء .

It is narrated: *"When the captives entered the city of Kufa,
which as we know from the history was in a state of desti-
tution, Lady Umm Kulthum was looking around. She was
weak, in need, in obvious pain and was exhausted from the
people of Kufa and what added to her grief was that she saw
them giving the children dates, fruit, bread and nuts at which
point Lady Umm Kulthum called out: 'Oh People of Kufa,
taking charity is prohibited for us!'. She then collected the food
from the children and threw it to the earth.
Musallam al-Jassaas said: 'When people saw this they started
to cry'.*

*At this point Lady Umm Kulthum again addressed the gath-
ering and exclaimed: 'Listen oh people of Kufa! Your men
are killing us while your women are crying for us! The judge
between us and you will be Allah on the Day of Decree'"*[1].

COMMENTARY

To illustrate the level of grief suffered by the Ahlul Bayt
(a) when they entered the city of Kufa, the narrator of
this *hadith* describes them as al-sabāyā translated as 'captives'. This word comes from sabb which in Arabic means
to 'curse' or 'abuse'. For example, the term is used in the
Holy Qur'an in the following verse: *"and do not abuse those
whom they call on besides Allah lest they wrongfully abuse
Allah out of their ignorance"* (6:108). This particular word

---

1 Bahrani, Hashim, *Awalim Sayida Nisaa*, vol. 2 #1015. Quoted in:
Shirazi, H., *Mawsu'atu Kamila (Kalimat Syeda Zainab)*, page 41

therefore indicates that the captives were not only prisoners of war, but that when they entered Kufa, they looked violated and abused.

This tradition raises a number of questions about why the family of the Prophet (s) are not permitted to accept charity and why Lady Umm Kulthum (s) threw away the food given to them when the children were in such a desperate state. One might wonder, what was the symbolic meaning of her actions?

Charity *(sadaqah)*, alms *(zakaat)* and one fifth of the year-end net-savings *(khums)* are the primary elements of the Islamic economic system; each have their own roles and associations. The importance of giving alms is mentioned in the Holy Qur'an extensively more than any other form of aid or donation and it is usually based on profit from any natural resource. Charity, however, is not limited to a set figure or a recommended amount; rather it is up to the individual to decide what they can afford to give away, and to whom they would like to donate. However, in the case of charity, the Holy Qur'an specifies the kind of people that qualify for this in the verse: "*Charity is only for the poor and the needy and the officials appointed to collect them, those whose hearts incline toward the truth and the ransoming of captives, those who are in debt, the cause of Allah and for the wayfarer. This is what has been ordained by Allah; indeed Allah is the All-Knowing and the Wise*" (9:60).

Although the Ahlul Bayt (a) and their blood descendants *(sadaat)*, could be included within these categories, they have a distinguished status and cannot therefore accept charity in this sense. Allah (swt) has elevated their position in the verse: "*Indeed Allah has chosen Adam, Noah, the family of Imraan and the family of Abraham above all people*" (3:33). The Ahlul Bayt (a) are the family of Prophet Ibrahim (a) and therefore just as Allah (swt) has raised their status above all creation, we must understand our servitude to the Ahlul Bayt (a) to be appropriate to their distinguished rank.

This law was introduced by the Holy Prophet (s) himself and has been frequently narrated in the books of traditions. For example, it is narrated that when Imam Hassan (a) was young, he took a date and put it toward his mouth and upon seeing this, the Prophet (s) told him "*Leave it! Leave it! Charity is not permissible for us*"[1]. Elsewhere it is also narrated that: "*Whenever the Prophet was presented with food he used to ask about it; if he was told it was a gift he would eat out of it and if he was told it was out of charity he would leave it*"[2]. Until today the *sadaat* will often check the source and intention of a gift when it is offered to them.

The provision made for the Ahlul Bayt (a), should they be in financial or material aid, is called *khums*. This is a levy of one fifth of the profit saved from the annual income, half of which is the proportion dedicated to the descendants *(sehme sadaat)* of the Ahlul Bayt (a). The Qur'an emphasises this right in the verse "*And know, whatever you gain a fifth of it is for Allah and the Messenger, for the near of kin and the orphans, the needy and the wayfarer if you believe in Allah and that which is revealed to our servant*" (8:41).

Khums is distinguished from *sadaqah* for a number of reasons. Firstly, charity is usually given to those who ask or beg for it, signifying a person's desperation and dire need for any amount of money or scrap of food that could be spared. The Ahlul Bayt (a) are forbidden from taking charity to detach them from these associations. If they are ever reduced to this situation, it is because the Islamic nation (*ummah*) has forgotten them or usurped their rights[3].

1   Ibn al-Hajjaj, Muslim, *Sahih Muslim*, book 5, hadith number 2339
2   Ibid, hadith number 2357
3   May Allah (swt) protect us from entering this state

Therefore, to avoid any embarrassment or indignity to the Ahlul Bayt (a), who are the sovereigns of this universe, and their descendants, Allah (swt) has provided them with a separate means for when they are in need.

Lady Umm Kulthum (s) was therefore following the command of Allah (swt) and the tradition of her grandfather when she rejected the charity offered by the people of Kufa. Lady Umm Kulthum (s) and her family were in heavy chains, their belongings plundered, surrounded by Imam Hussain's (a) killers, and paraded through the streets in which Imam Ali (a) used to distribute charity in the darkness of the night. Having seen their pitiful state, the women of Kufa offered whatever they could quickly distribute. Lady Umm Kulthum (s) stood tall to remind the congregation of their station, and that they must not be treated as beggars. By her very rejection of that charity, she was drawing the people's attention to the fact that they are from the noble family of the Prophet (s), to make them question the true identity of the women and children who had been shackled and humiliated.

Firstly, the narration demonstrates how the protection of the children was shared between Lady Zainab al-Kubra (s) and Lady Umm Kulthum (s). Imam Zain al-Abideen (a) was fighting a serious illness, and for large portions of the journey, he was still in a state of paralysing weakness. It is natural to say the daughters of Imam Ali (a) and Lady Fatima (s) would, in their selfless characters, be ready to sacrifice everything for the safety of their family members. However with their Imam (a) in such a state, an increased physical and emotional burden was placed upon their shoulders. In this state, there could only be two explanations why Lady Umm Kulthum (s), the younger sister and therefore with slightly differing responsibilities to her elder sister, would be at the forefront of the guardianship of the family. Either Lady Zainab (s) had asked her to take up this mantle, or she saw it necessary to relieve her elder sister due to her physical weakness. The first explanation indicates that Imam Zain al-Abideen (a) and Lady Zainab (s) trusted her ability to lead the group *(kaafila)* under these difficult circumstances. The second explanation shows that even though Lady Umm Kulthum (s) would have been exhausted from the journey, she not only recognised her sister's need for relief, but gathered enough strength and courage to take on that responsibility. In either scenario we are left overwhelmed by the leadership qualities demonstrated by Lady Umm Kulthum (s), and are reminded that she is indeed the daughter of the Commander of the Faithful.

The narration also highlights Lady Umm Kulthum's (s) knowledge of Qur'anic concepts and prophetic tradition. Furthermore, in refusing to allow the children to eat the dates and nuts from the people of Kufa or accept any form of charity, she cannot be considered as being cruel to the youngsters of the group who were in such need. Certainly, in their dreadful circumstances, taking this charity would have been permissible if it was needed to save their lives. The Holy Qur'an tells us: *"He has made plain what is forbidden to you, except that which you are compelled to"* (6:119). Rather, in refusing the charity from the people of Kufa, Lady Umm Kulthum (s) was exhibiting the peak of patience through difficulty. It also highlights her ability to judge the jurisprudential outcome of a situation. She judged the situation of the children, and assessed their needs while nurturing and looking after them as one of their main guardians after they were orphaned. As there was no need to accept the charity, she did not allow the children to eat the food. She not only had the knowledge and understanding of the rule of Allah (swt), she also had the poise and self-restraint to apply the knowledge in a situation to awaken the people of Kufa.

Lady Umm Kulthum (s) also used the opportunity to reprimand the people of Kufa. When deriding their actions she says "taqtulunā rijālukum" meaning *"your men are killing us"*. The heartbreaking context of this statement is that she referred to the situation in the present tense; if she had wanted to say "your men have killed us" using the past tense she would have said "qatalanā rijālukum". She was describing their *current* situation, not only of the martyrs left trampled and uncovered in the plains of Kerbala, but also the pitiful state of the ladies, children and Imam Zain al-Abideen (a), being dragged mercilessly from city to city in chains. By saying *"your men are killing us"* she declared to the world the extent of the torture and pain being inflicted by their captors, to the extent that they were on the verge of death. This was a warning to all participants and witnesses that not only did they have the blood of the men on their hands, but they were also about to commit the heinous crime of killing the women and children. Ultimately they did not heed this admonition as Lady Ruqayya (s), the young daughter of Imam Hussain (a), died in the prison of Yazid.

She added *"wa tabkīnā nisā'ukum"* which means *"and your women are crying for us"*. In the Arabic language, to change the diacritic movements *(harakaat)* of a word or even a single letter drastically alters the meaning of a statement. So if Lady Umm Kulthum (s) had said "wa tubkīnā nisā'ukum" her statement would have changed to 'your women are making us cry'. In this way, she tried to make the actions of both parties clear, as the Ahlul Bayt (a) were marched through the city in which she was once a princess.

She intended to convey what the men and the women, the husbands and their wives, fathers and their daughters were doing during their time of need. It is a statement asking the women of Kufa to realise who the cause of this dire state was. She also wanted them to reflect on their own reaction and responsibilities. Was it right that their own men were keeping the family of the Prophet (s) in chains whilst they were distributing scraps of food to the children, which they could not accept, and then weeping for them? She was asking, are you in turn weeping at the result of your and your own men's actions?

NARRATION 5: LADY UMM KULTHUM'S SERMON IN KUFA

قال : و خطبت أمّ كلثوم بنت عليّ عليه السلام في ذلك اليوم الذي أدخلوهم الكوفة من وراء كلّتها ، رافعة صوتها بالبكاء ، فقالت :

يا أهل الكوفة ، سوأة لكم ، ما لكم خذلتم حسيناً وقتلتموه وانتهبتم أمواله و ورثتموه ، وسبيتم نساءه ونكبتموه ، فتبّاً لكم وسحقاً .

ويلكم أتدرون أيّ دواة دهتكم ؟ وأيّ وزرٍ على ظهوركم حمّلتم ؟ وأي دماء سفكتموها ؟ وأيّ كريمةٍ أصبتموها ؟ وأيّ صبية سلبتموها ؟ وأيّ أموال انتهبتموها ؟ قتلتم خير رجالات بعد

النبيّ (ص) ، ونزعت الرحمة من قلوبكم ألا إن حزب الله هم

الفائزون ، وحزب الشيطان هم الخاسرون ثم قالت:

قتلتم أخي صبراً فويلٌ لأمّكم ستجزون ناراً حرُّها يتوقّدُ

سفكتم دماءً حرّم الله سفكها وحرّمها القرآن ثم محمّدُ

لفي سقرٍ حقاً يقيناً تخلّدوا ألا فابشروا بالنار إنّكم غداً

وإنّي لأبكي في حياتي على أخي على خير من بعد النبيّ سيولدُ

بدمع غزير مستهلّ مكفكف على الخدّ منّي دائماً ليس يجمدُ

قال الراوي : فضجّ النّاس بالبكاء والنوح ، ونشر النّساء

شعورهنّ ، ودعون بالويل والثبور ، وبكى الرجال ونتفوا لحاهم

فلم ير باكية وباكٍ أكثر من ذلك اليوم .

It is narrated: "*Lady Umm Kulthum (s) gave a sermon on the day in which they took her to Kufa. She was behind the cover of the carrier* [on the camel] *when she raised her voice while crying and called out:*

'*Oh people of Kufa! Shame on you! What is wrong with you, that you would discard Hussain? You murdered him and snatched away his property. You have taken his women as captives and you have tortured them. May you perish! May you despair! May you be taken to hell!*

Do you know what you have done? Do you know what crime you have committed? Do you know what weight you carry on your backs? Do you know which blood you have shed? Do you know which noble woman you have afflicted? Do you know which lady you have looted? Do you know what kind of wealth you have stolen?

You have killed the best man after the Prophet; the kindness has been taken away from your hearts! Know that the party of Allah are the successful, and the party of Satan are the losers'.

Then she said [in a poetic manner]: '*You have murdered my brother, may your mothers despair! You will be compensated with hellfire. You have shed the blood that Allah has forbidden you to shed, what the Qur'an has forbidden, then what the Prophet has forbidden. Now receive glad tidings that you will be in the hellfire and that tomorrow you will be in the worst of it; be sure that you will be in it forever! For surely I will cry my whole life for my brother, he was born as a righteous man after the Prophet. My tears are plenty, ever so heavy and flowing down my cheeks, they will never dry!*".

The narrator said: When the people [of Kufa] *heard this, all of them were wailing loudly and the women were pulling at their hair. They were calling out for the loss and destruction (to fall upon the Kufan people). The men wailed and tore at their beards. Nobody had seen more weeping people than on that day*"[1].

COMMENTARY

The narrator described Lady Umm Kulthum (s) as giving this sermon on the day she entered Kufa (al-yawm alladhī adkhalūhum). This means that it was delivered in

---

1 Ibn Tawus, *Al-Lahuf*, pages 67-68. Quoted in: Shirazi, H., *Mawsu'atu Kamila (Kalimat Syeda Zainab)*, pages 43-44

the streets and among the general public as opposed to in the court of the governor, Ibn Ziyad, which is where the majority of the other sermons were delivered. The books describing the tribulations after the event of Kerbala also mention similar sermons from Imam Zain al-Abideen (a), Lady Zainab (s) and Lady Fatima as-Sughra (s).

Lady Umm Kulthum's (s) sermon is fiery, yet astute and contains some of the most powerful insights about the events in Kerbala. She utilised key concepts from the Holy Qur'an and significant aspects of the prophetic narrations to turn the city of Kufa into a state of tumult. She openly displayed her anger and hostility toward the people of Kufa, showing no sign of sympathy or consideration for their apparent regret. Imam Ja'far as-Sadiq (a) narrates that his father Imam Mohammed al-Baqir (a) said that Lady Umm Kulthum (s) *"spoke to the people in the market of Kufa in which all the people remained silent. Then she gave a sermon so eloquently, it was as if it was Ali ibn Abi Talib speaking"*[1].

In normal circumstances it is not permissible to create public disorder, as this may be considered as a civil upheaval *(fitnah),* which is denounced in the Holy Qur'an in the verse: *"and fight them until there is no more disorder"* (8:39). How then do we understand the rebuke of Lady Umm Kulthum (s) toward the people of Kufa? The Holy Qur'an distinguishes between those who cause civil unrest through frivolous speech, and those who have the right to speak out. Lady Umm Kulthum (s) was seeking to address the very people that had invited her brother and promised him their allegiance and loyalty; it was her religious responsibility to remind the people of this. The Holy Qur'an discusses this concept in the verse: *"Allah does*

---

1 Shaheedi, Ja'far, *Fatima az-Zahr*a, page 257 (quoted from K*itab Balaaghat an-Nisaa'*)

not love the public utterance of hurtful speech, except by the one upon whom injustice has befallen" (4:148). This verse gives an exemption to people who are in need of telling the world what has happened to them. The family of the Prophet (s) had been treated unjustly, and so it was Lady Umm Kulthum's (s) right and responsibility to speak on their behalf, in the hope that her words would awaken the people of Kufa to the events, and shake them into realising the enormity of what had taken place.

The Holy Qur'an also describes that there have been people and communities that have committed the terrible act of killing a prophet of Allah (swt) in the following way: *"Utter shame is pitched over them, wherever they may be found. They have incurred the wrath of Allah and utter humiliation is pitched over them. This is because they rejected the signs of Allah, and slew the Prophets in defiance of right; this is because they were rebellious and transgressed all bounds"* (3:112). Imam Hussain (a) was a 'Sign of Allah (swt)' and the 'Inheritor of the Prophets'; his killing is akin to the killing of prophets and messengers. The part that the people of Kufa played in the killing of Imam Hussain (a) was significant, and so Lady Umm Kulthum (s) followed the Qur'anic instruction: *"as for those who deny the signs of Allah in defiance of right, slay the Prophets and slay those of mankind who enjoin justice, announce to them the most grievous penalty"* (3:21).

Lady Umm Kulthum (s) opens her speech by concisely describing how Imam Hussain (a) had been treated by the people of Kufa; she asked them *"What is wrong with you, that you would discard Hussain* (mā lakum khadhaltum Ḥusayna)?*"*. Her question is one of absolute disbelief and shock that they could desert their Imam (a) after faithfully writing thousands of letters promising him safety and security in Kufa. The root word of khadhaltum is khadhala or khidhlān which denotes the action of betraying or deceiving Imam Hussain (a). The translator here has used the word 'discard', because often in the Arabic language khidhlān is used to describe how a person might remove their ring or take off their shirt and throw it away without any concern. The Holy Prophet Muhammed (s) has used this term in his famous coronation speech at Ghadir Khumm when he formally announced the authority of Imam Ali (a). After he declared the famous words *"Whosoever master I am, Ali is his master too"* the Prophet (s) raised his hands and made a powerful supplication to Allah (swt): *"Oh Allah, befriend the one who befriends him, be the enemy of the one who is an enemy to him, help the one who helps him and discard the one who discards him* (wa ukhdhul man khadhala)"[1].

Lady Umm Kulthum (s) chose her words carefully. In one sentence she reminded the people of Kufa how they had discarded her father after the death of the Prophet (s), and how they had done the same to her brother, the inheritor and successor of her father. She was trying to warn the people that the prayer of the Prophet (s) for Imam Ali (a) also applied to Imam Hussain (a). She then described the physical and emotional torment that the women and children endured; she exclaimed: *"You have snatched away his wealth"* by using the words wa intahabtum amwālah. Intahaba or the verb nahaba means to 'snatch', but it refers specifically to an aggressive way to rob someone of their possession while they are still holding on to it. The victim is not capable of protecting themselves in a situation like this. Lady Umm Kulthum (s) then called out: *"May you perish!"* she said "fa tabban lakum wa suḥqā". She used the Qur'anic expression in the verse which addresses the enemy of the Prophet (s), Abu Lahab: *"Let the two hands of Abu Lahab perish and he himself will perish!"* (111:1). She

1 Ibn Hanbal, Ahmed, *Musnad,* vol. 4, page 281

also used the word suḥqā which means to 'send someone away' or 'vanquish them'; it is one of the most severe words in the Arabic language. It is used in the verse: *"Then they will confess their sin, so vanquished will be the dwellers of the blazing fire"* (67:11). In this way Lady Umm Kulthum (s) condemned the people of Kufa by likening them to the enemy of the Prophet (s) and the inhabitants of hellfire.

One of the most interesting statements Lady Umm Kulthum (s) made, is when she assessed the hearts of the Kufan people: *"The kindness has been taken away from your hearts!* (nuzi'ati al-raḥmatu min qulūbikum)!*". The word raḥma or 'mercy' in Arabic is the root of al-Raḥmān and al-Raḥīm[1] which are different aspects of kindness and compassion. Mercy, according to Allama Tabatabai in his commentary on the Qur'an, is *"when you see someone suffering, the reaction which you experience and that which tells you to provide for him that which he needs"*[2]. This mercy is therefore an all-encompassing trait that includes the qualities of sympathy and humanity. The Pharaoh at the time of Prophet Musa (a) was also described as devoid of any mercy and kindness. It is narrated that as a baby, Prophet Musa (a) was found in the River Nile and presented to the Pharaoh. His heart had become so dark and devoid of mercy that his first instinct was to kill the baby[3]. In a similar way, Lady Umm Kulthum (s) ascribed this position to the people of Kufa who attacked the helpless children of Imam Hussain (a), including his six month old son.

A significant aspect of Lady Umm Kulthum's (s) strategy was to distinguish the Ahlul Bayt (a) from the tyrants and their followers. She referred to the captured women as

---

1 Tabatabai, Mohammed Hussain, *Al-Mizan fī Tafseer al-Qur'an*, vol.1, page 26

2 Ibid

3 al-Majlisi, *Hayat al-Qulub*, vol. 1, page 301

'noble' women: "*Do you know which noble women you have captured?*", thereby distinguishing herself and the women of the family of the Prophet (s) from ordinary women. As she begins to conclude her speech, she returned to the Holy Qur'an to firmly establish the difference between the two groups. She said: "*Know that the party of Allah are the successful, and that the party of Satan are the losers*". The title 'party of Allah' or Ḥizb Allāh has been mentioned immediately after the verse of authority *(wilaayah)* [1] was revealed, announcing the position of Imam Ali (a) to the Holy Prophet (s) and Allah (swt)[2]. The verse says: "*And whoever takes Allah and His Messenger and those who believe as their guardians, then indeed the party of Allah, they are the victorious ones*" (5:56). The significant difference between Lady Umm Kulthum's (s) statement and that of the Holy Qur'an is the word used to describe the outcome of the 'party of Allah', for she calls them 'the successful' (fā'izūn), while the Holy Qur'an labels them as 'the victorious' (ghālibūn); it appears there are four reasons for this.

The first explanation is that Lady Umm Kulthum (s) did not want the people of Kufa to be confused about the meaning of her statement. The concept of victory in Kufan society was understood as worldly gain and victory in battle. Victory for the Kufans on the day of Ashura meant the defeat of Imam Hussain (a) and his army on the battlefield. Had they truly understood the meaning of victory in the Qur'anic sense, they would not have left the Imam (a) alone, and they would have understood that *they* were the real losers that day.

The second reason is that the verses of 'authority' and 'the party of Allah' are renowned parts of the Holy Qur'an, due to the reasons for revelation *(asbab al-nuzul)* and

---

1 Holy Qur'an (5:55)

2 Tabatabai, M.H., *al-Mizan*, vol. 11 page 7

their unique phraseology. Therefore it would have been likely that the crowd memorised these verses. Lady Umm Kulthum (s) may have decided to present a new interpretation of the verse to make them understand the verse and its implications. The word 'successful' (fā'izūn) has been used elsewhere in the Holy Qur'an, for example: *"In no way are equal the inmates of the fire and the companions of the garden; it is the companions of the garden that are successful"* (59:20). The 'party of Allah' are not only victorious, but it is their *actions* that grant them success.

Thirdly, it had only been 21 years since her father had been struck by a poisoned sword in the mosque in Kufa. It is likely that many people in the crowd had seen the Imam (a) and might have even witnessed the incident. Imam Ali's (a) famous words at that moment were *"I swear by the Lord of the Ka'ba, I have been successful"*[1]. These words would have been fresh in their minds. Lady Umm Kulthum (s) wanted to remind the people that the women in chains were the daughters of Imam Ali (a).

Lastly, the reason Lady Umm Kulthum (s) may have altered the final word from the original verse was to connect her next statement in the speech. Having declared that the *"party of Allah are successful"*, she adds that the *"party of Satan are the losers"*. Lady Umm Kulthum (s) drew on the themes of success and failure, which are used in the Qur'an to allude to the people of paradise who receive the best rewards from Allah (swt), and the people of hellfire who are in constant loss. The intriguing aspect of this word 'loss (khusr)' in Arabic is that it is the superlative form. This means that the 'loss' being described is not only the loss of personal and worldly belongings, but an intense and everlasting sense of loss. The Holy Qur'an mentions the term in a number of verses including: *"Shall we inform you of the*

---

1   Husayn, Ja'far, *Sirat Ameer al Mo'mineen*, page 708

greatest losers in their deeds? These are they who disbelieve in the communications of their Lord and His meeting, so their deeds become null" (18:103-105).

The term 'losers' (khāsirīn) has also been used by Prophet Adam (a) and Lady Hawwa (s) following their expulsion from the heavenly gardens. Although approaching the forbidden tree was not a sin, the displeasure of Allah (swt) was sufficient to tear the hearts of Prophet Adam (a) and Lady Hawwa (s) in overwhelming remorse. Imam Ali (a) described this feeling as being *"broken, apologising profusely, begging for forgiveness, abundantly repentant, acknowledging his deeds, utterly submissive and endlessly confessing"*[1]. Prophet Adam (a) and Lady Hawwa (s) regretted their mistake and called out: *"Oh our Lord! We have been unjust to ourselves and if you do not forgive us and do not have mercy upon us, then we shall certainly be of the losers!"* (7:23). Even though they had not committed a sin, they believed that their actions had caused a great distance between them and Allah (swt), that only begging for His divine mercy and forbearance could release them. Lady Umm Kulthum (s) tried to awaken the hearts of the Kufan people to realise what they had done, to regret and take account of their actions.

She conclusively revealed the station and outcomes of the 'party of Allah' and the 'party of Satan'. Through Qur'anic themes and expressions, Lady Umm Kulthum (s) ascribed every element of virtue to her family, and exposed the vile hearts and lowly consequences of those who butchered and enslaved her caravan. This is one of the most profound and powerful segments of her speech.

The next portion of her speech takes a different form. When she first addressed the crowd, Lady Umm Kulthum's (s) speech was powerful and admonishing. This is followed

1 al-Qummi, Abbas, *Mafatih al-Jinnan*, p167

by a swift change to a more poetic style. One might question how the change in style can be recorded in a narration; this can be discerned in a number of ways. Firstly, the narrator of the incident mentioned the change in style, therefore those who compiled the narrations have recorded it this way. Secondly in her sermon, her thoughts and arguments were expressed clearly; however, in her poetry she uses metaphors and similes as a descriptive and poetic tool.

The first line of poetry is one of the most heartbreaking lines regarding the event of Kerbala. She said: *"You killed my brother like an animal* (qataltum akhī ṣabran)". The word ṣabran used in the literal sense can be translated as 'slowly', altering the statement to: "You killed my brother slowly". Other translators have used the words 'cruelly[1]' and 'defenceless[2]'. Here the implied meaning is used, as the word is often used in Arabic to describe the scene or manner in which an animal is hunted. In either case, the Arabic language often uses the word ṣabran to mean a slow and lingering death; this is what happened to Imam Hussain (a) as described so tragically by his own sister.

Having offered this truly sorrowful introduction, she describes the result of their action as *"compensated by the hellfire"*. The word for 'compensated' used is satujzawna derived for jazā'. The Holy Qur'an uses the same language in the verse: *"Whoever does evil shall be rewarded with it accordingly"* (4:123). Even the type of hellfire she mentions, yatawaqqadu, has been described in the Holy Qur'an in the verse: *"He who has made for you the fire to kindle from the green tree, and behold! You will kindle it"* (36:80). There is an entire chapter of the Holy Qur'an dedicated to the people of *this* hell and the opening verses describe the traits of the people of Kufa: *"Woe to every slanderer, defamer. Who*

---

1 Munfared, *Imam Hussain and the Tragic Saga of Kerbala*, page 332
2 Ishtihardi, Mohammed, *Lamentations III*, page 25

amasses wealth and considers it a provision. He thinks that his wealth will make him immortal. Nay! He shall most certainly be hurled into the crushing disaster. And what will make you realise what the crushing disaster is? It is the fire kindled by Allah. Which rises above the hearts. Surely it shall be closed over, upon them. In extended columns" (chapter 104).

She continued: "Receive glad tidings that you will be in the hellfire (Fa abshirū fī al-nār, innakum ghadan la fī saqar). The word fa abshiru stems from fa abshir which means 'glad tidings', as in the verse: *"and give glad tidings to those who believe"* (2:223). This term is normally used in a positive or jovial connotation; however Lady Umm Kulthum (s) uses it ironically to emphasise the delusion of her enemies.

She also uses the word saqar which is a type of hellfire for specific people; the verse says: *"In the gardens, they shall ask of the guilty: what has brought you to this burning? They will answer 'we were not of those who prayed, and we did not feed the poor, and we used to enter into vain conversations with those who used to talk vainly, and we used to call the day of judgement a lie'"* (74:40-47).

By alternating linguistic expressions, her oratory style captured the people of Kufa. Through knowledge of the Holy Qur'an and wondrous eloquence, she demonstrated that she is the daughter of the Commander of the Faithful and the Leader of the Women of Paradise. The poetic language Lady Umm Kulthum (s) used allowed the people of Kufa to picture their own destiny, as she often used words that have either Qur'anic connotations or symbolise a severe repercussion; both of which were designed to leave the onlookers pondering their own destiny. The result of this was to put the capital of the Muslim nation into a state in which they *"had never seen before"*.

Narration 5: Lamentation Upon Entering Medina

لَّا عاد أهل البيت من سبيهم واقتربوا من مدينة جدّهم رسول الله
(صلّى الله عليه وآله) توجّهت أم كلثوم إلى المدينة وجعلت تبكي
وتقول:

فبالحسرات والأحزان جئنا	مدينة جدّنا لا تقبلينا
بأنا قد فجعنا في أبينا	ألا فاخبر رسول الله عنا
بلا رؤوس وقد ذبحوا البنينا	و أن رجالنا بالطفّ صرعى
و بعد الأسر يا جدّا سبينا	و أخبر جدّنا أنّا أسرنا
عرايا بالطفوف مسلّبينا	و رهطك يا رسول الله أضحوا
جنابك يا رسول الله فينا	و قد ذبحوا الحسين و لم يراعوا
على أقتاب الجمال محملينا	فلو نظرت عيونك للأسارى
عيون النّاس ناظرة إلينا	رسول الله بعد الصون صارت
عيونك ثارت الأعدا علينا	و كنت تحوطنا حتى تولت
بناتك في البلاد مشتتينا	أفاطم لو نظرت إلى السبايا
و لو أبصرت زين العابدينا	أفاطم لو نظرت إلى الحيارى
ومن سهر الليالي قد عمينا	أفاطم لو رأيتينا سهارى

أفاطم لو رأيتينا سهارى   ومن سهر الليالي قد عمينا

أفاطم ما لقيتي من عداكي   و لا قيراط ممّا قد لقينا

فلو دامت حياتك لم تزالي   إلى يوم القيامة تندبينا

و عرج بالبقيع وقف وناد   أيا ابن حبيب رب العالمينا

و قل يا عم يا حسن المزكى   عيال أخيك أضحوا ضائعينا

أيا عمّاه إن أخاك أضحى   بعيدا عنك بالرمضاء رهينا

بلا رأس تنوح عليه جهرا   طيور والوحوش الموحشينا

و لو عاينت يا مولاي ساقوا   حريما لا يجدن لهم معينا

على متن النياق بلا وطاء   و شاهدت العيال مكشفينا

مدينة جدنا لا تقبلينا   فبالحسرات والأحزان جئنا

خرجنا منك بالأهلين جمعاً   رجعنا لا رجال ولا بنينا

و كنا في الخروج بجمع شمل   رجعنا حاسرين مسلّبينا

و كنا في أمان الله جهراً   رجعنا بالقطيعة خائفينا

و مولانا الحسين لنا أنيس   رجعنا والحسين به رهينا

فنحن الضائعات بلا كفيل   و نحن النائحات على أخينا

و نحن السائرات على المطايا   نشال على جمال المبغضينا

و نحن بنات يس وطه   و نحن الباكيات على أبينا

و نحن الطّاهرات بلا خفاء   و نحن المخلصون المصطفونا

و نحن الصابرات على البلايا   و نحن الصادقون الناصحونا

ألا يا جدّنا قتلوا حسينا   و لم يرعوا جناب الله فينا

ألا يا جدّنا بلغت عدانا   مناها واشتفى الأعداء فينا

لقد هتكوا النّساء وحملوها   على الأقتاب قهرا أجمعينا

و زينب أخرجوها من خباها   و فاطَمْ والهٌ تبدي الأنينا

سكينة تشتكي من حرّ وجدٍ   تنادي الغوث ربّ العالمينا

و زين العابدين بقيد ذلٍ   و راموا قتله أهل الخؤونا

فبعدهم على الدنيا تراب   فكأس الموت فيها قد سقينا

و هذي قصّتي مع شرح حالي   ألا يا سامعون ابكوا علينا

It is narrated that: "*The Ahlul Bayt returned from their time in captivity and when they reached closer to Medina, the city of their grandfather the Holy Prophet, Lady Umm Kulthum began to cry loudly and recited:*

'*Oh city of our grandfather, do not accept us! We have come to you with deep sorrows and regrets.*
Ah! Inform the Messenger of Allah about us, that the great calamity befallen us after our father.
And that our men are all dead, left in Kerbala, without their heads and that all the children were slaughtered.

And inform our grandfather that we were captured and were
robbed of everything; that your people were sacrificed,
left bare in Kerbala and were persecuted.
And they slaughtered Hussain without consideration of your
status toward us; if only you could have seen the captives on
the backs of the camels.
Oh Messenger, after all of these hardships, the eyes of the
people stared at us and if you could only have understood
what we saw and how the enemies were torturing us.
Oh Fatima, if only you could have seen your daughters as
captives, you would have seen us scattered; if only you could
have seen your followers and could have seen our Zain
al-Abideen.
If only you could have seen us at night and from being
awake all night, we became blind! What you have seen befall
us from your enemies is not even a share of what has truly
happened to us.
If your life would have continued you would have mourned
us until the Day of Judgement! So go, ascend to al-Baqi and
stand and announce, oh the son of the beloved of our world!

And say, oh uncle, oh my dear Hassan the Pure, the children
of your brother, they have been sacrificed and they have
vanquished us. Oh uncle, surely your brother, most certainly
sacrificed well away from you.
He was left without a head and circled by the wild birds and
beasts that were frightening us; if only you could have seen,
oh my master, they took the women and we could not find
anyone to help us.
We were on top of the camels without a cover, and you would
have found your family members bare.
Oh city of our grandfather, do not accept us! With sorrows
and grief we came. We left you with all the family members
together and return to you without men and without sons;

when we went out we were all united, we came back bare and looted. We were under Allah's public safety and came back abandoned and full of fear.

And our master Hussain, he was for us a comfort; we came back while Hussain became a hostage. For us now, we are lost without a guardian; now we are mourning our sorrows for our brother.

We will continue to go after those who were hating us, for we are the daughters of Ya Seen and Taha; we will continue to cry for our father.

We are the ones who are pure without hiding it and we are the ones who have been made righteous; we are the ones who are most patient during a calamity and we are the most truthful and the best of advisers.

Ah! Oh Grandfather! They killed Hussain, they did not pay attention to the status Allah has given us.

Oh our Grandfather! The enmity reached to such an extent! And the enemies transgressed upon us, they deprived us and took us all by force.

And they took Zainab out of her covering and they hid our belongings; Sakinah was so troubled by the hot weather crying 'save us, oh Lord of the worlds!' and Zain al-Abideen was in a very heavy chain!

They threw the dead and scattered the bodies; after them, the world is like dust for we have drunk from the glass of death.

This is our story and our situation – Oh who are listening, cry profusely for us!"[1]

COMMENTARY

The poetry recited by Lady Umm Kulthum (s) on the approach to her grandfather's city is one of the most famous accounts regarding the Ahlul Bayt's (a) release from

---

1 al-Majlisi, *Bihar al-Anwar*, vol. 45, pages 197-198

imprisonment. It is often recited by scholars and poets, specifically over the *Arba'een* period commemorating forty days after the day of Ashura.

The lamentation recounts the tragedy that befell Lady Umm Kulthum (s) and the family of the Prophet (s) and provides insight into the extent of their devastation and trauma. The narration also increases our awareness of the contribution Lady Umm Kulthum (s) has made to Islamic history; her praiseworthy status; and her linguistic capabilities.

For those who are able to read the Arabic text, the rhythm and rhyme of each verse flows poetically; each line ends with the pronoun nā which means 'us' in Arabic. The words roll off the tongue effortlessly in all thirty eight stanzas. Without practice or rehearsal, this spontaneous outburst of bereavement is both emotional and truthful. This elegy is therefore considered to be one of the wondrous acts of Lady Umm Kulthum (s).

One may reflect upon how it is possible for Lady Umm Kulthum (s) to possess such abilities. The first element to consider is the importance of poetry in the Arab society of that period and its usage. Poetry, in the pre-Islamic and post-revelatory period, was considered to be a necessary skill in the Arab society. Reputations were built on poetic achievements and great respect was commanded by the lead poets of the time. It was used regularly on the battlefield to portray bravery and valour against the enemy, and to describe an event that has taken place. For example, there was an annual competition when poets from across the land would travel to Makkah to present their poems; the one voted the best had the honour of hanging their poem on the door of the Holy Ka'ba until the following year's contest. The Holy Qur'an often refers to the use of poetry by the Holy Prophet (s); for example it says: *"And we have not taught him poetry; nor would it have suited this message, rather it* [the Qur'an] *is a reminder and a divine discourse"* (36:69). Here Allah (swt) distinguishes between the words of revelation and the poetic words of man. Some argue that it is due to the Arab society's love for literature and poetry that Allah (swt) appealed to them with the miracle of the Qur'an; in the same way as He sent Prophet Musa (a) with the miracle of magic, and Prophet Isa (a) with the miracle of medicine: to reach the people of their times, respectively.

The Holy Qur'an is replete with examples of metaphors, similes, rhythm and rhyme, indicating its poetic nature. Each verse in the chapter of The Moon (chapter 54) ends with the letter ra and each verse of the chapter of The Sun (chapter 91) ends in the letter hā; the chapter of The Beneficent (chapter 55) presents the question *"Which of the favours of your Lord do you now deny?"* alternating a span of 65 verses; and the chapter of The Spider (chapter 29) uses the metaphor of a spider's web to speak of the fragility of this world. These are but a few examples.

This literary miracle had a tremendous effect on the people who wrote and heard poetic compositions of the highest technique and fluency; they were then presented with words of a divine nature. For example it is narrated that Tufayl Ibn Amr, whose melodious poetry earned him great respect from his tribe, came to Makkah. The chiefs of the Quraysh gathered around him to sow the seeds of enmity towards the Prophet (s) and said: *"That man who is offering his prayers by the side of the Ka'ba has destroyed our unity, and created dissensions amongst us by his magical narrations, and we are afraid that he will create a similar discord in your tribe too".* Tufayl recounted that: *"Their words impressed upon me so much, that fearing Muhammad's magical words might affect me, I decided not to speak to him.*

In order to ward off any influence I put some cotton in my ears while performing the circumambulation around the Ka'ba, so that his voice could not reach me while he was reciting the Qur'an and offering prayers. In the morning I entered the Holy Mosque and was not expecting to hear him speak, however, I don't know what happened that all of a sudden some extremely sweet and charming words reached me. Upon hearing this I said to myself 'Curse be upon you! You are an eloquent and intelligent person, what is the harm if you listen to what this man says? If he says something good you should accept it, otherwise you can very well reject it'".

Tufayl continued to explain: *"I waited in such a way that I would not contact the Prophet openly. At last the Prophet proceeded to his house and he entered it. I followed and obtained permission and entered the house too. I told him the entire story and said: 'The Quraysh ascribe so many things to you and in the beginning I had no intention of seeing you. However, the sweetness of the Qur'an has drawn me to you. I now request that you kindly explain to me the nature of your religion and recite a portion of the Qur'an to me'".*

He concluded: *"The Holy Prophet made known to me his religion and recited some verses of the Qur'an. By God! I had never heard a narration more appealing"*[1].

The impact of the immaculate words of the Qur'an is on account of them being revealed from the Creator and Sustainer of the universe. This is a significant factor in understanding how Lady Umm Kulthum's (s) words could have impacted the people of Medina with her poetry. Her poetry mirrored the Qur'anic style, ending in the same letter in each verse, and there is no doubt that she possessed the spiritual gifts directly from the Creator of these words. In a Hadith al-Qudsi[2] Allah (swt) says: *"Oh son of Adam!*

---

1 Subhani, Ja'far, *The Message*, chapter 18, pages 252-253

2 'Hadith al-Qudsi' is a narration from Allah (swt)

Obey Me in that which I have asked you to obey Me and refrain from that which I have asked you to refrain from to the extent you will be able to say to something 'be' and it will be"[1]. The key point in this, and in many similar narrations, is that Allah (swt) has promised to make His submissive servants 'like Himself'. Allah (swt) is 'the Speaker *(al-Mutakallim)*[2]'; He spoke to Prophet Musa (a) through a burning bush; and is the creator of language itself who *"taught (man) the mode of expression"* (55:4). He is the perfect speaker who grants the gift of eloquent speech to those who serve Him. This is the first way to appreciate how Lady Umm Kulthum (s) could compose incredible poetry.

Secondly, the gift of divine eloquence of speech had been bestowed to the Ahlul Bayt (a). The Holy Prophet (s) was granted a tongue purified from any defect. The Holy Qur'an says: *"nor does he speak out of his own desire. It is nothing except inspiration"* (53: 3-4). This was manifested in every statement and conversation with the Prophet (s) and thus earned him the titles 'the truthful *(as-Saadiq)*' and 'the trustworthy *(al-Ameen)*' from his peers in Makkah prior to the period of revelation.

Lady Umm Kulthum (s) also inherited the linguistic capabilities of her father, Imam Ali (a), and mother, Lady Fatima (s). Although Qur'anic verses were not revealed to them directly, they reflected the Holy Prophet's (s) attribute of purity of speech. They demonstrated this in many ways: Lady Fatima's (s) famous speech in the Prophet's (s) Mosque, when she addressed the Caliph Abu Bakr and presented arguments to defend her right to keep the land of Fadak, is one example. The people of Medina were as-

1   Shirazi, H., trans by Baqri, Z., *al-Hadith al-Qudsi*, page 30

2   Whilst this title cannot be found in the Holy Qur'an, its root and usage has been mentioned in (4:164), (6:115), (7:137) and (11:119); see also: Kho'i, Abul Qasim, *The Prolegomena to the Qur'an*, chapter 13, page 268

tonished by her oratory skills and clarity of her arguments. To illustrate this, below is a section from her speech:

The narrator said: *"She [Lady Fatima (s)] opened her speech by glorifying Allah and by sending salutations to the Prophet of Allah. Then she consoled the people for their crying over her situation. When they stopped crying she continued her speech and said:*

الْحَمْدُ لله على ما أَنْعَمَ ، وَلَهُ الشُّكْرُ على ما أَلْهَمَ ، وَالثَّناءُ بِما قُدَّمَ مِنْ عُمومٍ نِعَمٍ ابْتَدَأها ، وَسُبُوغِ آلاءٍ أَسْداها وَتَمامِ مِنَنٍ أُولاها جَمَّ عَنِ الإِحْصاءِ عدَدُها ، وَنأى عَنِ الْجَزاءِ أَمَدُها ، وَتَفاوَتَ عَنِ الإِدْراكِ أَبَدُها ، وَنَدَبَهُمْ لاسْتِزادَتِها بالشُّكْرِ لاتِّصالِها ، وَاسْتَحْمَدَ إلَى الْخَلائِقِ بِإِجْزالِها وَثَنّى بَالنَّدْبِ إلى أَمْثالِها.

وَأَشْهَدُ أَنْ لا إلهَ إلاَّ اللهُ وَحْدَهُ لا شَرَيكَ لَهُ ، كَلِمَةٌ جَعَلَ الإِخْلاصَ تَأْوِيلَها وَضَمَّنَ الْقُلُوبَ مَوْصُولَها ، وَأَنارَ في التَّفَكُّرِ مَعْقُولَها الْمُمْتَنِعُ مِنَ الإِبْصارِ رُؤْيَتُهُ وَمِنَ الْأَلْسُنِ صِفَتُهُ وَمِنَ الْأَوْهامِ كَيْفِيَّتُهُ ، ابْتَدَعَ الْأَشْياءَ لا مِنْ شَيْءٍ كانَ قَبْلَها ، وَأَنْشَأَها بِلا احْتِذاءِ أَمْثِلَةٍ امْتَثَلَها كَوَّنَها

'Praise belongs to Allah for what He has blessed and all thanks to Him for what He has inspired. And I am thanking Him for what He created amongst His general blessings and the bounties He has decorated upon them.

He created the differences in His mercy and He commanded His creatures to seek more blessings by showing Him gratitude. And Allah created the tendency of gratitude in them and then Allah thanks those who are running after gratitude.

I bear witness that there is no God except Allah and that Muhammad is His messenger. In this declaration, sincerity is its true interpretation and He guarantees its acceptance to the heart and He enlightens the thoughts.

The eyes comprehend Him not and the tongues cannot describe His attributes. Opinions cannot depict Him. He is the one who innovated all things; He was there when there was nothing before Him and He created things without anything before Him"[1].

This speech was extensive in its duration and evolved into a debate with the Caliph Abu Bakr over Qur'anic verses, prophetic narration and the science of jurisprudence. It was an impromptu response to the oppression the Ahlul Bayt (a) had faced since the death of the Holy Prophet (s), in front of the dominant members of her community. In the Arabic text, every stanza concludes in rhyme.

This extract clearly demonstrates that Lady Fatima (s) was the daughter of the one endowed with revelation. In the same way, Lady Umm Kulthum's (s) lamentation at the gates of Medina was a reflection of her mother's words. In terms of its fluency, use of the Arabic language, rhyme, Qur'anic referencing and intensity, the lamentation is in every way identical to that of her blessed mother's, and therefore it is clear that Lady Umm Kulthum (s) inherited her grandfather's and mother's gift.

Her father, Imam Ali (a) is also well known for his literary achievements and unparalleled discourses. The scholar, Syed Sharif ar-Radhi compiled hundreds of his sermons,

1 Khafajee, *Maqatil al-Ma'sumeen*, page 115

letters and instructions into a book entitled *Nahjul Bala-gha*, '*The Peak of Eloquence*'; a testament to his oratory style. There are numerous examples of the most articulate speeches; one in particular is entitled 'A Sermon Without Dots'[1]. The Arabic alphabet comprises of twenty eight letters of which fifteen are letters with dots. It is therefore considered extremely skilful to conduct a sermon without using any word which contains a letter with dots. This can only be explained in view of the tradition of Imam as-Sadiq (a): *"Knowledge is not achieved through learning, rather it is a light that descends into the heart of the one whom Allah the Almighty wishes to guide"*[2].

Considering the accomplished nature and content of the Holy Qur'an, the luminous personality of the Prophet Muhammad (s), and the piercing insight possessed by Imam Ali (a) and Lady Fatima (s), it is of no wonder that Lady Umm Kulthum (s) produced such poetry. She was immersed in the company of these oceans of pure knowledge at all times, and as her father stated: *"Your tongue will urge you to say whatever you have accustomed it to say"*[3].

Lady Umm Kulthum (s) addressed the city of her grandfather *('madinatu jaddina')*, and not the inhabitants of the city. She asked for the city not accept them, as if to say 'how can you accept us in this state, having left with the very people who made your city so noble and now return to you so forlorn?'. To address the city, which is by its nature an inanimate group of buildings and structures would normally be considered peculiar; however, its root and true connotation can be found in the Holy Qur'an, with a profound message from Lady Umm Kulthum (s).

---

1   al-Shafi'I, Muhammad Ibn Muslim, *Kifayat al-Talib*, page 248; see also, Ibn Abi al-Hadeed, *Sharh Nahj al-Balaghah* vol. 19, page 140

2   al-Majlisi, *Bihar al-Anwar*, vol. 1, page 225, hadith number 17

3   Amidi, *Ghurar al-Hikam*, hadith number 7634

The story of Prophet Yusuf (a) has been recounted in chapter twelve of the Holy Qur'an. It addresses the jealousy of his brothers and their plot to rid themselves of him; it outlines his encounters with the wife of the *Aziz*, his time in prison and his eventual release to become the Minister for Agriculture and the Treasurer of Egypt[1]. The story reaches the point when the brothers return home from Egypt without Benjamin, Prophet Yaqub's (a) favourite son after Prophet Yusuf (a). When Prophet Yaqub (a) saw that the brothers had returned home without Benjamin after promising to look after him, the brothers said: *"Oh our father! Your son committed theft and we do not bear witness except to that which we know and we could not keep watch over the unseen"* (12:81). Knowing the impeccable character of Benjamin, Prophet Yaqub (a) could not believe that he would commit such a crime and responded *"My son is not a thief!"*[2].

Faced with their father's stance the brothers then decided to resort to another means of convincing him of what they saw, and told him to *"ask the town and the caravan with which we returned and you will find we are indeed telling the truth!"* (12:82). The brothers are appealing for their father to *"ask the town"* or *"the caravan"* in the same way as Lady Umm Kulthum (s) addressed the *"city of her grandfather"*; both appeal to inanimate places or objects. What the brothers meant by their appeal was 'ask the *people* of the town' who were also witness or 'the *people* of the caravan' whom they were travelling with. The Holy Qur'an often uses this style of language to present a point, for example in the verse: *"As for these towns, we destroyed them when they acted unjustly"* (18:59). The town *itself* did not act unjustly, rather it was the *people* of the town who acted

---

1 For further information, see al-Majlisi, *Hayat al-Qulub*, vol. 1, page 237

2 al-Majlisi, *Hayat al-Qulub*, vol. 1, page 263

unjustly and therefore it was they who were destroyed by Allah (swt). This style of language is called 'phatic communication', where words or phrases that have a social function are applied without the cause of inferring the literal meaning. In this way, when Lady Umm Kulthum (s) directed her speech to the city of her grandfather, she is in fact addressing the residents of the city and telling them *"not to accept"* her return.

From another perspective, Lady Umm Kulthum (s) is using the backdrop of this verse to present a concise and demonstrative message. In the conclusion of the verse in the chapter of Yusuf, the brothers proclaimed that their statements should be verified by the people of the caravan who actually witnessed the cup being pulled from Benjamin's bag, to testify that they had told the truth and that Benjamin was a thief. The implied meaning of this statement is that verification from the number of people who had witnessed the occasion first-hand, would convince any person that the brothers were truthful in their claims. Lady Umm Kulthum (s) presented a similar argument to the people of Medina: if you want to know what intolerable crimes took place on the day of Ashura, ask us, the Ahlul Bayt (a). This call can be appreciated on three levels. Firstly, Lady Umm Kulthum (s) was making an implicit call to the people of Medina, and the Muslim nation to ask about what happened to her brother, Imam Hussain (a), his companions and his children. The Ahlul Bayt (a) were keen to spread the message of Imam Hussain (a). Secondly, it was important for those who witnessed the tragedy to make people aware of the events of the day of Ashura in order to avoid exaggerations and misrepresentations[1]. Lastly, it was important to make these events well-known

---

1 For further information, see: Mutahhari, Murtaza, *Ashura: Misrepresentations and Distortions*

in order to prevent sceptics from denying that the event took place. There were many extraordinary occurrences throughout the journey: the earth trembled and the skies rained blood for several days immediately after the martyrdom of Imam Hussain (a). It was important to the Ahlul Bayt (a) that these calamities were not turned into myths and legends. Lady Umm Kulthum's (s) message was that if someone wants to know what happened in Kerbala, they should refer to those people who were first-hand witnesses.

Lady Umm Kulthum (s) goes on to tell the people of Medina to: *"inform the Messenger about us"* and *"inform our grandfather that we were captured"*. These appeals are quite intriguing considering the Holy Prophet (s) knew of all the events that would take place. It is reported that he came to Umm Salama and Abdullah Ibn Abbas (a) in a dream to inform them of the imminent demise of Imam Hussain (a). One of the endeavours beyond the words of this request was for the people of Medina to recall the bond between the Holy Prophet (s) and his grandson, Imam Hussain (a). They would have seen how the Prophet (s) loved his grandchildren and proudly said *"Hussain is from me, and I am from Hussain"*[1]. Therefore, her words were not literal, but explained that Imam Hussain (a) was the beloved of the Prophet (s), and they should send their condolences to him and reaffirm their pledge of allegiance to the Ahlul Bayt (a).

Lady Umm Kulthum continued her elegy by describing some of the greatest tragedies that befell the Ahlul Bayt (a). Among them she states that: *"we were robbed"* and left *"bare in Kerbala* ('Arāyā bi al-Ṭufūfi musallabīnā)". The word 'Arāya denotes the garments that were worn, and musallabīnā is from the root salaba which means some-

---

1 Ibn Maja, *Sunan*, vol. 1, page 56; see also Ibn Hanbal, Ahmed, *Musnad*, vol. 4, page 172

thing that is taken by force. This is in particular reference to the heartbreaking plunder of the Imam (a), as his body lay on the sands of Kerbala. It is narrated that: *"Ishaq Ibn Hawayh took away his shirt and Bajdal cut off his finger in order to take away his ring"*[1]. Following this, a group of men approached, and each looted something from his possession after which one man stated: *"I wanted to remove his [the Imam's] undergarments but he had put his right hand on it which I could not lift off, so I severed his right hand off. He then put his left hand on it which I also could not lift so I severed his left hand off. It was then that I heard something like an earthquake, so I became frightened and left him"*[2].

Having addressed the townsfolk and asked them to recount the tragedy to her grandfather, Lady Umm Kulthum (s) addresses her mother by calling out *"Oh Fatima!"*. Under normal circumstances, this would have been perceived as poor etiquette. However, this proclamation was again intended to remind the people of her lineage, and rather than calling out 'Oh mother', she emphasised the great name of Lady Fatima (s). Her name had now become synonymous with grief and tragedy. She had repeated this aim by also mentioning her brother, Imam Hassan (a) by name.

Lady Umm Kulthum's (s) words to her mother seem very deliberate, indirectly conveying this message to the people of Medina. She described their ordeal and the sequence of events that took place, the night following the day of Ashura, the periods in prison, and their return to their home. When she recounted the first night in captivity, she described the family as mushattatīnā, which is derived from the root shatta or to be 'separated'. It is possible that she is portraying their separation from the martyrs

---

1 Ibn Tawoos, *Al-Lahuf*, page 73
2 Ibn Shahr Ashub, *Manaqib*, vol. 2, page 224

who remained in Kerbala. However, the narrations of the first night and the ransacking of the tents describe how the women and children were forced to flee in any direction to save themselves from the raging fires and beatings of the raiders.

Lady Umm Kulthum (s) continued to address her mother by describing the period of imprisonment as being so severe that *"being awake all night"* caused them to become *"blind"*. This is not in the literal sense, such as when Prophet Yaqub (a) mourned the separation from his son Prophet Yusuf (a) (12:84), rather it is a poetic expression of the family's intense state of grief.

Approximately half way through the address, Lady Umm Kulthum (s) repeated the opening line of her poem: *"Oh city of our grandfather, do not accept us!"*. This was deliberate as there are two very distinct themes in the poem. The first half focused on the calamities that befell the family; this may have been because it was aimed at introducing the story of Kerbala to the whole city, so that there would be no person unaware of the details of what transpired. The second half concentrated on the outcome of these tragedies, such as the Ahlul Bayt's (a) beleaguered and fraught condition. Interestingly, Lady Umm Kulthum (s) began to approach the subject of the aftermath of Kerbala and the next steps that the Ahlul Bayt (a) were planning to take. For example, among the declarations about the state of the family is the phrase *"we are lost without a guardian* (Fa naḥnu ḍā'i'āt bi lā kafil)". The word kafil is synonymous with someone who takes responsibility for another or becomes their guardian. This word is often mentioned when a person applies for a Hajj visa and is required to declare who their kafil is. The Holy Qur'an uses this word to describe Prophet Zakariyya (a) as the guardian of Lady

Maryam (s), in the verse which says Allah (swt) *"gave her into the charge of Zakariyya"* (3:37). Using this word, Lady Umm Kulthum (s) described her situation without her protector, Imam Hussain (a). The poet Syed Mohammed Hussain al-Kishwani composed the following words regarding this loss:

> *"And a woman cried from the side of her tent*
> *She lost her protector, beating her cheek she kept.*
> *The whips hurt her, so she under them bends;*
> *She cries, and her voice oft*
> *Causes even the stones to get soft.*
> *She was carried on lean beasts in captivity*
> *From a place to place displayed as booty.*
> *She went away led by asses: Umayyad,*
> *From one apostate to another she was led"*[1].

There are three verses where Lady Umm Kulthum (s) imparted the strategy of the Ahlul Bayt (a) to continue the message of Imam Hussain's (a) mission. She said *"Now we are mourning our sorrow for our brother. We will continue to go after those who were hating us. Oh who are listening, cry for us!"*. Lady Umm Kulthum (s) used the word al-nāʾiḥāt translated as 'mourning'; this is a very expressive word used to describe the style of narrating their tribulations to the world. Its root is the word nāḥa and from this, other languages such as Urdu, have derived the word nawḥah, which is the melodic recitation of elegies depicting the oppression and tragedies of the Ahlul Bayt (a). Lady Umm Kulthum (s) advised the people not to forget the message of Imam Hussain (a) and emphasised the importance of recounting the incident of Kerbala. This was a tremendously powerful message emanating from one of the leaders of

1 al-Muqarram, *Maqtal al-Husain*, chapter 52, hadith number 71

the household, and someone who had the responsibility of propagating the message of Kerbala to the whole world.

This style of remembrance developed into dedicated mourning sessions led by the Ahlul Bayt (a), where poets and narrators were invited to recount the sufferings of the family. For example Abu Haroon al-Makfoof narrated: *"I presented myself before Imam as-Sadiq, he said to recite poetry for him and thus I began. He said 'not in this manner, recite the poems in the way you do over the grave of Hussain and so I did for him"*[1]. He continued to recite: *"'While passing by the grave of Hussain tell his blessed bones...'. Then the Imam started weeping and hence I became silent. Imam as-Sadiq told me to continue and recite some more, thus I recited 'Oh Farwa! Arise and weep and lament upon your Master Hussain, give an opportunity to weep over the corpse of Hussain'. Abu Haroon continued saying that Imam as-Sadiq wept bitterly and the women of his household wept too"*[2].

Lady Umm Kulthum (s) also instructed all those who were listening and all those who would eventually receive her words to *"cry for us"*. Here Lady Umm Kulthum (s) emphasised the significance of not only attending mourning sessions for the Ahlul Bayt (a), but also crying for their sorrows and suffering. There are numerous traditions detailing the reward for a person who expresses grief over the sufferings of the Ahlul Bayt (a). For example Imam ar-Ridha (a) said: *"Whoever remembers our sorrows, and weeps over the oppressions which have been inflicted upon us, then on the Day of Judgment, he shall be on our status along with us. And the one who remembers our sorrows and weeps and makes others weep, then his eyes shall not weep on the day when all eyes will be weeping. And the one who sits in such a gathering when our matters are discussed, his heart will not*

1 al-Majlisi, *Bihar al-Anwar*, vol. 44, page 287
2 al-Qummi, A., *Nafas al-Mahmoom*, chapter 3, section 2, hadith 2

die on the day when all hearts shall perish"[1]. Furthermore, Imam Zain al-Abideen (a) said: *"If a believer weeps over the martyrdom of Imam Hussain and tears flow from his eyes and fall on his cheeks, then Allah will make him reside in the palaces of paradise where he shall abide for a lengthy period of time. And if tears flow from a believer's eyes and fall upon his cheeks for the oppression and tyranny which has been inflicted upon us by our enemies, then Allah will present him a seat in paradise. And the believer who undergoes sufferings on our behalf and tears flow on his cheeks, then Allah will remove sorrow from his face, and on the Day of Judgement will keep him away from His wrath and safeguard him against the fire of hell"*[2].

The instruction to hold these mourning sessions has a meaning beyond the apparent, and the result of them is beyond the rewards mentioned. Lady Umm Kulthum's (s) aim was not only to ensure the people of Medina were aware of Imam Hussain's (a) martyrdom, but that they became aware of the underlying causes of his movement against the leadership of the time. In this way they could generate support and unity for his mission. The gatherings and lamentations were a means to this end, and gave the Ahlul Bayt (a) an opportunity to draw the Muslim nation *(ummah)* closer to them through awareness, love and adherence. For example, Imam as-Sadiq (a) met with his companion Fudhayl and asked: *"Do you sit together, talk and discuss amongst yourselves?"* Fudhayl replied *"Yes"*. The Imam (a) then said: *"I approve of these sittings, so keep our issue* [divinely appointed leadership] *alive. May Allah exhibit mercy on those who revive our issue and mission!"*[3].

---

1 Ibid, hadith number 6; see also al-Majlisi, *Bihar al-Anwar*, vol. 4, page 178

2 Ibid, hadith number 11

3 Al-Amili, Hurr, *Wasa'il as-Shi'a*, vol. 10, page 391

This address from Lady Umm Kulthum (s) can be described as her single most important contribution to the history of Islam. It is an eloquent yet stirring address to the community, that heralded the place and period of revelation. It speaks to all parties of the Muslim nation *(ummah),* past and present; its content catalogues the adversities the Ahlul Bayt (a) had to endure, while setting out a clear programme for reform in the community. Most importantly, it was perhaps the first public elegy regarding the tragedy of Kerbala that the people of Medina had heard. It is this elegy that has led generation after generation of mourning gatherings around the world, that have remained the cause of the survival and reestablishment of the religion of Islam. Lady Umm Kulthum (s) had the honour of initiating this process that remains the heartbeat of the religion today, and will continue until the end of time.

Her Death

Having lived under the care, love and wisdom of seven Infallibles, from the Prophet Muhammad (s) to Imam Mohammed al-Baqir (a), Lady Umm Kulthum (s) had witnessed all that Islam had achieved and fallen foul to. She had witnessed the revelation of the Holy Qur'an and the divine leadership of the Imams (a). However, she also witnessed the peak of moral degradation and man's ability to trudge through the darkest regions of the soul.

The Holy Qur'an identifies with people of her blessed nature when it states: "*And We will most certainly try you with something of fear and hunger and loss of property and lives and fruits; give good tidings to the patient. Who, when a misfortune befalls them, say 'Indeed we belong to Allah and unto to Him shall we indeed return'. Those are the people upon whom are blessings and mercy from their Lord and those are the followers of the right course*" (2:155-157).

It is narrated that "*when Lady Umm Kulthum reached Medina, she again began challenging the Ummayid family in order to change the opinion of the people. She (s) often conducted gatherings for women explaining to them the details of the revolution just as Lady Zainab used to do*".

Among the large gatherings that she held, she stood up and recited a poem recounting what they had faced in Kerbala, on the way to Kufa and on the way to Damascus. After she finished the people cried a lot and cursed the Umayyid family. It is for this reason she was bestowed the title of *Umm al-Nawaha* or 'the mother of lamentations'[1].

This news spread and the governor of Medina put Lady Umm Kulthum (s) under house arrest and stopped people from going to the house - especially when they saw numerous delegations sending their condolences – but the house arrest did not stop her from exposing the atrocities of the Umayyid family and for their crimes in Kerbala and capturing the women. She continued to challenge without fear until she became sick from fatigue and the lasting effects of the tragedy. The sickness did not take long until her death was announced"[2].

After more than fifty years of submitting entirely to the Will of Allah (swt) and exhibiting every noble characteristic, she had completed her mission and fulfilled her responsibilities, and was to return to her Lord awaiting the greatest of rewards.

Regrettably, just as historians cannot agree the exact date of Lady Umm Kulthum's (s) birth, neither can they be certain of the date of her death and burial ceremonies. Helpfully, there is only one recorded time of death for Lady Umm Kulthum (s), and historians unanimously agree that *"she died four months and ten days after returning to Medina"*[3]. This is ambiguous because there are varying opinions on the exact date that the caravan returned to Medina.

1 Baydhoon, L., *Mawsu'atu Kerbala*, vol. 2, 640

2 Zumaizan, Saeed Rasheed, *Nisaa al-Hawla al-Hussain*, pages 55-56

3 Khafajee, Abd al-Ameer, *Maqatil al-Ma'sumeen*, page 307; see also al-Muhajir, Abd al-Hamid, *I'ilamu annee Fatima*, vol. 3, page 2; Ibn Abi al-Hadeed, *Sharh Nahj al-Balaghah*, vol. 2, page 475; al-Amini, *A'yaan ash-Shi'a*, vol. 7, page 126; Al-Anba, *Umdat at-Talib*, page 54

According to some time lines, the family of the Prophet (s) returned to Medina on the 20th of Safar 61 AH; this would calculate the date of her death to be the 1st Rabi' at-Thani 61 AH. However, the majority of historians believe that the 20th of Safar is the date of their arrival back to Kerbala to bury the heads of the martyrs[1] and fulfil mourning ceremonies which lasted for three days[2]. The problem here is that the historians who propose this do not provide a definitive return date to Medina[3]. There are, however, recorded travel times for the caravans of the time. For example, using the recorded information that the Holy Prophet (s) left the city of Medina for the farewell pilgrimage in Makkah, approximately a 200 mile journey, he left on the 28th of Dhul Qa'da[4] and arrived on either the 4th or 5th of Dhul Hijjah[5], which illustrates that the journey from Medina to Makkah took approximately one week. It is also known that Imam Hussain (a) left Makkah on the 8th of Dhul Hijjah[6] and arrived in Kerbala on the 2nd of Muharram[7]. This shows that an 800 mile journey was covered in three and a half weeks. From this information it can be concluded that a caravan would cross a distance of approximately 30 miles a day.

This being the case, the journey from Kerbala back to Medina would have been approximately 600 miles; it would therefore take the caravan 20 days to reach the city of their grandfather and their home. The historians who say that the family of the Prophet (s) arrived in Kerbala on

1 Munfared, *Imam Hussain and the Tragic Saga of Kerbala*, page 403

2 *Dhorri'a al-Najaat*, page 271. Quoted in: Munfared, A., *The Tragic Saga of Kerbala*, page 406

3 For more information, see: Tabatabai, Qadhi, *Research about the 40th of Imam Hussain*

4 Subhani, Ja'far, *The Message*, page 741

5 Ibid; see also *Sahih Muslim*, vol.1, page 402

6 at-Tabari, *Tareekh at-Tabari*, vol. 6, page 177

7 al-Baladhuri, *Ansaab al-Ashraaf*, vol. 3, page 385

the 20th of Safar and stayed for three days before returning to Medina, would therefore calculate the date of their
arrival in Medina to be on the 10th of Rabi' al-Awwal 61
AH. If Lady Umm Kulthum (s) passed away four months
and ten days after her return to Medina, the date of her
death, using these calculations, would be on the 20th Rajab
61 AH. Interestingly, Lady Zainab (s) is recorded to have
passed away on the 15th of Rajab a few years later.

Despite her noble position and accomplishments
within the Holy Household, it appears there is no mention
in the books of history or the biographies of Imam Zain
al-Abideen (a) of the direct cause of her death or the burial
ceremonies that took place. However, the physical hardship she endured throughout the journey from Kerbala to
Kufa and Damascus, including her thirst and hunger in
the desert heat, the chaffing chains that tied her for many
days, and the pain of constant lashings finally took their
toll. This relentless torture, accompanied by the grief for
her brother and family members, is an unparalleled burden
on any human. Lady Umm Kulthum (s) would have been
approximately 55 years old and would have suffered a great
deal of weakness even after her return. One explanation
of why there are no records of her burial ceremony is that
she may have requested to have been buried at night or in
secret just like her mother and father.

There is a shrine dedicated to the remembrance of
Lady Umm Kulthum (s) in the cemetery known as *Baab
al-Saghir* in Damascus[1], the city where Lady Zainab (s)
is also thought to have been buried. There are also some
who believe that as Lady Zainab (s) died and was buried in

---

1 Baab al-Saghir is the name of the street which has cemeteries on
either side of it, the cemetery have therefore become popularly known
as 'Baab al-Saghir Cemetery'

Egypt[1] and that the grand and noble shrine in Damascus actually contains the blessed tomb of Lady Umm Kulthum (s)[2]. However, it is difficult to prove that Lady Umm Kulthum (s) travelled back to Damascus after her return to Medina, as there is no historical record to verify this. It can therefore be concluded that Lady Umm Kulthum (s), like many members of the Ahlul Bayt (s) and noble companions, is buried in the precincts of *Jannat al-Baqi*, the cemetery adjacent to the mosque of the Holy Prophet (s), alongside her blessed brother Imam Hassan (a) and three other infallible Imams (a).

Some believe that Lady Zainab (s) is also buried there[3], however there is evidence to suggest that she died in Damascus. However, it is possible that these reports refer to Lady Zainab as-Sughra (s), that is, Lady Umm Kulthum (s). Indeed Allah (swt) knows best.

---

1 Shahin, Badr, *Lady Zainab*, page 220

2 For differing opinions see: Ibrahim, Muhammad Zaki, *Maraaqid Ahl al-Bayt fil Qaahira*; Ibn al-Hourani, *Ziyarat*; al-Mousili, al-Ma'aref

3 Shahin, Badr, *Lady Zainab*, page 219

Raising Awareness of Lady Umm Kulthum

There are a number of reasons why Lady Umm Kulthum (s) is considered to be the forgotten member of the household of the Prophet (s), they include uncertainties regarding her existence and the lack of composite material recorded about her character. This has led to her absence from library bookshelves and remembrance programmes dedicated to her legacy.

The aim of this book is to address these issues and analyse all the relevant information available about her life, and the peripheral issues that have shaped our understanding of her character and circumstances. By thoroughly examining her movements and achievements, this book is the first step to redress these issues.

The question now is, what do we do with this material? Should these efforts be publicised in the hope that the message will reach her followers? Should it be relegated to library shelves and used only by scholars for reference purposes? This would not befit her message. The very purpose of this effort is to raise the position of Lady Umm Kulthum (s) to the station she deserves. Therefore, what strategy can be presented to help achieve this aim?

As an Individual

Firstly, it is important to be thankful to Allah (swt) for her existence, for it is a mercy for us to know her as an intercessor, a helper, and as one of the foremost female role models in Islam. This is something that has been recommended to us in the Holy Qur'an, when it states: *"And Muhammad is no more than a Messenger; the Messengers before him have passed away. If then he dies or is killed will you then turn back on yourselves? And whoever turns back on his heels by no means harms Allah; and Allah will reward the thankful"* (3:144).

Secondly, taking time to consider our individual responsibility toward Lady Umm Kulthum (s) is a valuable experience. This action is highly recommended to do in regard to the Awaited Saviour, Imam al-Mahdi (a) (may Allah (swt) hasten his reappearance), as pondering over one's role in his absence will help to motivate a person to act in his way. Similarly, it is important to think and ponder over the verses of the Qur'an, the message of the Prophet (s) and the members of his Holy Household, because it is only through *thinking* that internal reformation can take place.

The more we ponder, the more we find that each holy personality in Islam represents their own element of struggle; they have their own part to play in history that must be intrinsically understood and emulated. The Ahlul Bayt (a) are *"alike and unalike"*[1]; Imam as-Sadiq (a) is by nature as holy a personality as Imam al-Hadi (a); their personas, aims and divine stations are the same. Indeed the Holy Prophet's (s) family *"are like stars, which ever of them you follow you will be guided"*. The difference was in their method of presenting the message, the particular trials they had to face and the legacies they left behind for us to learn from.

1 For further information on this subject, see: as-Sadr, Mohammed Baqir, *Ahl al-Bayt Tanawwu' Ahdaf wa Wahdah Hadaf*

From this perspective, Lady Umm Kulthum (s) has something unique to offer. We can ask ourselves: What does Lady Umm Kulthum (s) stand for? What spiritual relationship do I have with her? What unique message does she portray beyond the unified message of the ladies of Ahlul Bayt (a)? What about her which was previously hidden is now apparent? In what way do I most identify with the plight of Lady Umm Kulthum (s)? How can she best be represented? How many years of ignorance toward her right am I in need of recounting? If she asked me to dedicate one good deed to raise her status in the community, what might that be? How can I, with my personal skill set, best serve Lady Umm Kulthum (s)? Ultimately, the answers we draw will be entirely personal, relative to our capabilities and understanding of her.

The reward for pondering on these and many more related questions are beyond the scope of this book. These reflections will no doubt result in a spiritual migration towards her and other members of the Ahlul Bayt (a); from understanding the basic historical details about her life to building an attachment to her personality in the heart. The natural effect of this relationship is to turn to her as a means of seeking our needs before the Almighty Creator and Sustainer. The Holy Qur'an demands this of us in the verse: *"Oh you who believe! Have God-consciousness and seek a means of nearness, strive hard in His way so that you may be successful"* (5:35). Lady Umm Kulthum (s) is one of the means to seek nearness to Allah (swt). She can be approached as an intermediary to present a need before Allah (swt), be it a spiritual, physical or material. We can also fervently ask whatever we desire through the right and love of a personality who is supremely elevated in spiritual standing.

The books of supplication often teach the method and etiquettes of approach. These include beginning and ending with salutations and blessings on the family of the Prophet (s), and recounting the tragic moments of her life, particularly the times in Medina, Kerbala and Damascus while crying for her loss and suffering. It is also important to remember to pray for the Imam (may Allah hasten his reappearance) of our time, family, friends, the deceased, the sick, the community, scholars, the people around the world and our own needs, all through the name and wondrous status of Lady Umm Kulthum (s).

When a member of a family or a close friend passes away, it is a common spiritual practise to offer a gift to them, which is usually a good deed on behalf of the *marhum* (deceased believer). The gift can be anything from recitations of the Holy Qur'an to a pilgrimage or a fast. It is narrated separately by both Hammad Ibn Uthman and Umar Ibn Yazid that Imam as-Sadiq (a) said: *"One who performs a deed on behalf of a dead believer, he is rewarded twice that by the Almighty Allah and the departed one is also grateful to him"*[1]. It is also narrated that the person receiving is aware of the one who sent the gift, as Hisham Ibn Saalim, a companion of both Imam as-Sadiq (a) and Imam al-Kadhim (s) narrated that Imam [as-Sadiq (a)] was asked whether *"Supplication, charity, fasting and similar things reach the dead? If so, does he know who has sent it to him?"* To which he replied *"yes"* to both questions[2].

Certainly the rewards of these good deeds reach the person they are intended for, and the person who gives the gift is also rewarded for his good action. However, have we considered doing the same for the Ahlul Bayt (a)? It is nar-

---

1   Al-Amili, Hurr, *Wasa'il as-Shi'a*, vol. 5, page 369, hadith number 24 and 25

2   Ibid, page 366, hadith number 7

rated that the Awaited Saviour, Imam al-Mahdi (may Allah hasten his reappearance) said: *"One who gifts the reward of his* [supplementary] *prayers to the Messenger of Allah, the Commander of the Faithful, Ali Ibn Abi Talib and the Imams after him, Allah shall increase the reward of this prayer to such an extent that one would become breathless while counting it. And before his soul is separated from his body he is told 'Oh Man, your gift has reached me! Since this is the Day of Recompense that Allah has fixed for you and which you have reached; congratulations for it!'"*[1]. Here, the recipient of the gift is not in need of the reward or prayer that a devotee offers, it is the person who gives the gift that benefits.

The aim of bestowing gifts of good deeds such as prayers and recitations to Lady Umm Kulthum (s) is not to attempt to increase her reward with Allah (swt), rather it is an expression of pure love and devotion towards her. By remembering her and acting in her way, a believer can hope that she will intercede for them in the fulfilment of their needs, and remember them on the day when no one will be allowed to intercede except by the permission of Allah (swt). According to the recommendations, there are some particular words that can be recited after the prayer or the giving of any gift: *"Oh Allah, these two sets of prayer are a gift from me to the most purified and chaste Umm Kulthum, the (grand)daughter of your Prophet (s). Oh Allah, please accept them from me and convey them to her from me and reward me with the best of that which I hope from you, your Prophet, the successor of your Prophet, Fatima Zahra the daughter of your Prophet, Hassan and Hussain, the grandsons of your Prophet and the protectors from the progeny of Hussain. Oh guardian of the believers, oh guardian of the believers, oh guardian of the believers!"*[2].

---

1 Ibn Tawus, *Jamaal al-Usbu*, page 493
2 Ibid, page 15; see also Isfahani, M., *The Perfection of Morals Among*

Our personal relationship with Lady Umm Kulthum (s) should not stop there. A believer should take lessons from her life and desire to reflect her righteous qualities, with the knowledge that she is pleased with their actions. Imam Zain al-Abideen (a) describes this in his 'Whispered Prayer of the Devotees' when he says: *"Join us to Your servants, those who hurry to You swiftly, knock constantly at Your door, worship You by night and by day while they remain apprehensive and in awe of You! You have purified their drinking places, taken them to the objects of their desire, fulfilled their requests, accomplished their wishes through Your bounty, filled their minds with Your love and quenched their thirst with Your pure drink. I ask You to place me among those who have the fullest share from You, the highest station with You, the most plentiful portion of Your love and the most excellent allotment of Your knowledge"*[1].

Every description and quality mentioned is certainly manifested in the holy personality of Lady Umm Kulthum (s). In this supplication, the Imam (a), who is himself purified, is begging Allah (swt) to unify him with people who have these characteristics; we too should be begging Allah (swt) for this opportunity.

The Imam (a) mentions this request in many ways, in his supplications. In the 'Whispered Prayer of the Lovers':

"Oh My Lord! Place us with him who You have chosen for Your nearness and friendship, who You have purified through Your affection and Your love, who You have given the yearning to meeting with You, who You have made pleased with Your decree, who You have allowed to gaze upon Your face, who You have shown the favours of Your pleasure, who You have given refuge from separation from Yourself, who You have settled in

---

the Benefits of Praying for al-Qaim, vol. 2, page 366

1   Qarashi, *The Life of Imam Zain al-Abideen*, pages 481-482

a place close to Your neighbourhood, who You have singled out for true knowledge of Yourself, who You have made worthy for worshipping Yourself, whose heart You have made captivated with Your will, who You picked for contemplating over Yourself, whose look You made empty except for Yourself, whose heart You have freed for only Your love, who You have made desirous of only what is with Yourself, who you have inspired with Your remembrance, who You have allotted to give constant thanksgiving to Yourself, who You have occupied with obeying Yourself, who You have turned into the most righteous of creation, whom You have chosen to whisper to You and from who You have cut off all things which has cut him from You. Oh My Lord! Place us among those whose habit is rejoicing in You and constantly yearning for You, whose time is spent sighing and moaning; their heads are bowed, prostrating before your might, their eyes are wakeful in Your service, their tears are flowing in dread of You, their hearts are fixated upon Your love and their cores are shaken in absolute awe of You"[1].

The unification that Imam Zain al-Abideen (a) speaks of in his prayer is a bond that begins in *this world*. The bond with these personalities is a bond with their attributes, to everything that is good. This association with these holy personalities is what might save us.

The Holy Qur'an explains that there are some people who have fulfilled their covenant with Allah (swt) and have submitted completely to His command: *"And do not consider those who have died in the way of Allah as dead; Nay they are alive! It is only that you do not perceive it* (2:154). Allah (swt) speaks of people whose lives were manifestations of the highest traits, they lived and died purely for His pleasure and part of their reward is a spiritual presence felt in this world.

---

1 Ibid, pages 481-482

The role of the Ahlul Bayt (a) is to help us achieve what Allah (swt) expects from us as human beings, as the best of His creation. This aim, in the light of the previous verse, does not change after they pass away. Lady Umm Kulthum (s) is of the Ahlul Bayt (a). She is of a purified status; her life was entirely dedicated to the service of Allah (swt) and thus she too is spiritually alive and exists to provide us with the necessary guidance; it is entirely our responsibility to knock at her door.

There are many examples of the spiritual masters achieving this state of cognition and unification with those they cherish the most. For example, Ayatollah Ibrahim Amini (may Allah grant him a long life) narrates that he was present in the room on the last night before Allama Syed Mohammed Hussain Tabatabai was taken to the hospital where he passed away. He said: *"After an hour he* [Allama] *regained consciousness and sat on his bed for approximately 45 minutes. In the same state as he was in before, he stared at the corner of the room and then fell asleep. After some time when he woke up he moved from his position as if he wanted to get up. We asked him, 'do you want to get up?' He said 'Those two individuals that I was waiting for have come' and stared at the corner dazzled and astonished"*[1].

This unification is something that should be earnestly sought after, day and night, in every state and in every action. We should ponder over the exquisite personalities the Ahlul Bayt (a) have, how they are the manifestations of absolute perfection, and even to share a moment in their divine presence would be indescribable. If we can, for a moment, even grasp the pure light that Lady Umm Kulthum (s) is, we would work diligently to sit, for just a moment, with our heads humbly bowed in her presence.

---

1 Luqmani, *Eternal Manifestions: 80 Stories from the Life of Allama Tabatabai*, section 16, story 4

As a Community

The Holy Qur'an demands that a dual approach be observed in everything we do. In the chapter of Time (chapter 103) in the Holy Qur'an, Allah (swt) tells us: *"Most surely man is in loss. Except for those who believe and perform good deeds and call others toward the truth and toward patience"*. In these verses Allah (swt) presents the idea that we have both personal and social responsibilities. For example, the spiritually focused discussion on connecting with the pure light that is Lady Umm Kulthum (s) is a very personal matter; the Holy Qur'an says *"whoever goes aright, does so only for the good of their own soul"* (17:15) clearly indicating that actions are primarily for our own selves; however Islam also demands that we look beyond just our own lives and consider our role as part of a society.

Islam is concerned with man's social responsibilities and emphasises that those who understand their actions and have an effect toward bettering the community are described as *"a good seed that sprouts"* (48:29)*;* whilst there are others who *"inspire people to varnish falsehood"* (6:112) and *"harm people out of their ignorance"* (49:6).

Therefore our responsibilities toward Lady Umm Kulthum (s) also have a social connotation; we must raise her status across the Muslim nation *(ummah)* and beyond. This too requires a strategy and recommendations.

Firstly, it is important to include Lady Umm Kulthum's (s) birth and death anniversaries in our religious calendars in the same way as other members of the Ahlul Bayt (a). In this way, the name of Lady Umm Kulthum (s) will be well recognised within the Muslim nation. In addition, communities around the world can hold gatherings to celebrate and commemorate these anniversaries each year. In this way Lady Umm Kulthum (s) would become an established fixture in the remembrance programmes around the world and at least twice a year. Communities spanning the globe would be given the opportunity hear of her nobility, history, spirituality, struggles, maxims and lessons.

In the Holy Qur'an, Allah (swt) has promised a great reward for those who encourage others to do good actions: *"Whoever recommends and helps a good cause will become a partner to it"* (4:85). Becoming *"a partner"* to the cause is when a person begins a tradition of a good action, it is often embraced by other people and continues from one generation to the next. Similarly if one programme organiser establishes the remembrance of Lady Umm Kulthum (s), that person will receive the reward each time the community holds that programme, for as long the programme continues.

The question arises that although a relatively accurate death date can be established for Lady Umm Kulthum (s), the date of her birth is still controversial. Ultimately, the date commemorated does not need to match the accurate historical date; what is important is that a day is set aside to thank Allah (swt) for her birth, to speak about her noble characteristics and to think of practical ways to implement her lessons in our daily lives. One suggestion is to celebrate her birth on the 16th of the month of Ramadhan, a day after the birth date of Imam Hassan (a). Although this date is not widely recorded, it might be considered a preference due to its timing in the Islamic calendar. Whatever date is chosen, ensuring her remembrance flourishes in the communities of the world should be our priority.

The second way that a community can seek to raise the status of Lady Umm Kulthum (s) is to request scholars to speak about her life, especially during the times of Muharram, Safar, the month of Ramadhan, and when visiting the cities of Damascus, Kufa, Kerbala and Medina, all of which are associated directly to her life. Just as this book was an initiative which stemmed from the encouragement of Haji Mohammed, the demand from hundreds of thousands of people who visit these cities in honour of the Ahlul Bayt (a) each year by questioning their guides and scholars regarding her life and achievements will kindle a greater awareness of her.

Lastly, when a daughter is born in the community, we can consider naming her 'Kulthum'. Throughout history the Banu Umayyah have attempted to eradicate the name of Ali Ibn Abi Talib (a) by publicly denouncing his name at every Friday sermon and even offering a financial reward to forget the name 'Ali'. The Ahlul Bayt (a) opposed this, naming their children after Imam Ali (a). In fact, three other Imams (a) are named Ali, they are: Imam Ali Zain al-Abideen (a); Imam Ali ar-Ridha (a) and Imam Ali al-Hadi (a).

The remembrance of Lady Umm Kulthum (s) has always been in the hands of the followers of the Ahlul Bayt (a). Just as we take responsibility for the lack of material available about her life, we can also take responsibility for changing this situation. The ideas presented are by no means comprehensive, and as we continue to discover more treasures in the libraries of the world, and as technology advances, we should develop more ways of dedicating our love toward her.

Conclusion

Among the themes presented in this book is the unique position of Lady Umm Kulthum (s). She has been a figure frequently forgotten in history and is often overlooked by all schools of thought.

Over time she has become increasingly disregarded by the Muslim nation; the ambiguity over her existence and life became prevailing matters of discussion, as opposed to emphasis on her achievements and maxims. This resulted in a vast degree of contradiction and contrasting views on the diminutive number of narrations which have been recorded about her.

Some questioned her very existence and whether she was, in reality, the same person as her elder sister Lady Zainab (s). This theory stemmed from the lack of recorded biographical information, and that she shared both the same name and epithets as her sister. While the merits of the scholars asserting these arguments are of lofty repute, their argument does not constitute as sound evidence against her existence. Rather the sheer volume of original and authentic sources narrating that there were two sisters, who performed separate actions and had individual merits undoubtedly establishes Lady Umm Kulthum (s) as the second daughter to Imam Ali (a) and Lady Fatima (s).

The importance of confirming Lady Umm Kulthum's (s) existence should not be underestimated, as this appears to be the main reason for the lack of significant research about her accomplishments. As the scholars of the forthcoming generations assume the responsibility of publishing written works for their era, and adopt the role of guides to the holy visitation sites, they can utilise this work as a foundation to build on. To this end, this book has attempted to shed light on her noble characteristics and suggests that she should be adopted as a role model for the Muslim nation, as her devotees would already trust in her piety, chastity and knowledge. A further aim of this book was to recount her understanding and application of Qur'anic concepts and verses from her speech and poetry. Some examples include her confrontation with Hafsa, her sermon in Kufa and the lamentation she recited upon entering Medina.

The second element of her life that has been heavily debated is the view that she married the second Caliph, Umar al-Khattab. Historians have scrutinised the evidence for many marriages based on their purpose and outcome; however, this marriage is perhaps the only one that has caused a divide between Shi'a scholars. While the idea of her marriage to Umar would be considered abhorrent by the Shi'a nation, the vast majority of scholars from the 4th to 10th century AH believe the marriage took place under duress. During this period some scholars presented opposing views, and as supplementary evidence was gathered it became more appropriate to reject the authenticity of the narrations of their marriage.

Lady Umm Kulthum (s) is not only considered unique because of these controversial issues, but it is the particular lessons we can learn from her personality and circumstance that differentiate her from other members of the Holy Household (a).

She can be considered as a test for the entire Muslim nation; a trial from Allah (swt) of our love and efforts towards the Ahlul Bayt (a). Although many Muslims pride themselves on the devotion they exhibit to the Holy Prophet Muhammad (s), the Holy Qur'an also instructs the believers to extend this commitment to members of his Holy Household (a): *"I do not seek any reward, except for love for my near relatives"* (42:23). As there is a distinct lack of material dedicated to Lady Umm Kulthum (s), it is our responsibility to fulfil the message of this verse in our own way and in our own capacity. The Holy Qur'an says: *"We test you all through the bad and good things of life by means of a trial* [for you]" (21:35). The verse implies that our test before Allah (swt) may not be in the form we expect it to be. The more our awareness of the Ahlul Bayt (a) grows, the greater our responsibility toward them. Therefore Lady Umm Kulthum (s) presents an open challenge to the Muslim nation, and particularly the Shi'a community, of our dedication and love towards her by grasping and appreciating every aspect of her life.

Lady Umm Kulthum (s) is also unique in that she presents a challenge for the scholar. Each student of Islam, whether researching privately or under the tutorship of an institution must be adept at such technical sciences such as *Ilm al-Rijal*, deducing the reality of historical contradictions, demonstrating independent and sound reasoning, knowledge of intrafaith dialogue and the ability to construct a debate.

There is a distinct lack of debate over the births, deaths, marriages and movements of other members of the Ahlul Bayt (s). Their maxims are cited and sermons recorded in thousands of volumes in libraries around the world. However, all these issues in the life of Lady Umm Kulthum (s) are disputed and debated. From one perspective, this may be considered a burden, but for the diligent and truth-seeking scholar it is not a dilemma, but a pleasure and honour to wade through the books of history, untangle well-established arguments, and shine light on the life of a personality who had given every breath in service of the message of her grandfather.

From another perspective, the scholar must be trained to challenge and be challenged. While the vast majority of subjects regarding the Ahlul Bayt (a) are agreed upon, the blessing from Allah (swt) to us may be a personality that we must *strive* to understand.

Ultimately both of these unique challenges were presented to Imam al-Khomeini. In the introduction to this book, the story of how Lady Umm Kulthum (s) presented herself to Imam al-Khomeini was mentioned. She complained of the neglect she had faced. His reaction, both as a member of the Muslim nation and as a principal scholar was to perform research about her life and mention her name and noble characteristics whenever he had the opportunity. For example on October 31st 1978, in his residence of *Neauphle-le-Chateau* in Paris, he discussed the qualities of leadership and forms of government with a group of students. He stated: *"On the eve of Hazrat Amir's death, the night on which he was struck a blow, he is said to have been a guest in the home of Umm Kulthum and on being brought salt and milk by his daughter with which to break his fast, asked her when she had ever seen him eating two kinds of food on the same occasion. When the Hazrat then told his daughter to take one of the two foods away she was about to remove the salt; the Hazrat is said to have implored her to take away the milk instead. He then took two morsels of the bread and salt and ate them"*[1].

The beauty of this story is that it encapsulates the entire

---

1 *Al-Kauthar*, vol. 2, page 363

message of this work: Lady Umm Kulthum (s) was over-looked; she made herself known; she was sought after and then spoken of.

How then do we summarise Lady Umm Kulthum (s)? Should we focus on the oblique or obscure aspects of her life? Ayatollah Shaheed Mohammed Baqir Sadr (a) stated in his last public communication before being murdered *"the life of any being is not measured except by how much he can give to his ummah, by his presence, his life, his thought"*[1].

Lady Umm Kulthum (s) lived in the presence of seven Infallibles and reflected their light in every action she performed. Through her proximity to Imam Ali (a) and Imam Hussain (a) she embraced their struggles as *her* struggles, leaving us an eternal legacy matched by no person other than her sister Lady Zainab (s).

There is now no reason for her to be considered as the hidden treasure. She is *our* treasure.

---

1 http://www.youtube.com/watch?v=9NQW88y_lBo[Accessed on 03/01/11]. For further quotes from Shaheed as-Sadr see: Burhani, Haider Bilal, *Qasas wa Khawaatir min Hayaat as-Shaheed as-Sadr*

Bibliography

Ibn Abd al-Barr, *al-Istiab fi Ma'rifat al-Ashaab*, Dar al-Kutub al-Ilmiyya, Beirut, 1995.

Imam Ali Ibn al-Hussain, Zain al-Abideen, *A Divine Perspective on Rights*, Ansariyan Publications, Qom, 2002.

Amidi, A., *Ghurar al-Hikam*, Mu'assasat al-Aalami, Beirut, 1987.

al-Amini, M., *A'yaan ash-Shi'a*, Dar al-Ta'aruf, Beirut, 1986.

Ibn Athir, *al-Kamil fi Tareekh*, Dar al-Sadir, Beirut, 1982.

al-Baghdadi, Ibn Sa'd, *Tabaqat al-Kubra*, Dar al-Ihyaa turath al-Arabi, Beirut, 1996.

al-Baladhuri, A., *Ansaab al-Ashraaf*, Dar al-Fikr, Beirut.

Baydhoon, L., *Mawsu'atu Kerbala*, Mu'assasatu al-A'lami lil Matbu'at, Beirut, 2006.

Hamadani, A., *Fatima Zahra Bahjatu Qalbi Mustapha*, Nashr al-Mardhiya, Qom, 1372 HS[1].

Ibn Hanbal, A., *Musnad, al-Maktab al-Islami*, Beirut, 1993.

al-Hilali, Ibn Qays, *Kitab-e-Sulaym*, S.& N. Rizvi, UK, 2001.

al-Hindi, M., *Kanz al-Ummal*, Mu'assasat al-Risalat, Syria, 1403 AH[2].

---

1 HS refers to the solar years after the *hijra*

2 AH refers to the lunars years after the *hijra*

Husayn, J., *Sirat Ameer al-Mo'mineen*, Ansariyan Publications, Qom, 2006.

Isfahani, M., *The Perfection of the Morals among the Benefits of Praying for al-Qaim*, vol. 2, Ja'fari Propagation Centre, Mumbai, 2009.

Ishtihardi, M., *Lamentations II*, Al-Mahdi Institute, UK, 2001.

Ishtihardi, M., *Lamentations III*, Al-Mahdi Institute, UK, 2005.

Jaffer, M., *Lady Fatima Masuma (a) of Qum*, Jami'at al-Zahra, Qom, 2003. http://www.al-islam.org/masumaqum [Accessed on 27 October 2011]

al-Kaashi, A., *at-Tareeq ila Mambr al-Hussain*, Dar al-Hawra, Beirut, 2010.

Ibn Kathir, *al-Bidaya wan-Nihaya*, 1988, Dar al-Kutub al-Ilmiya, Beirut and 1990, Maktaah al-Ma'arif, Beirut

Al-Kauthar, The Institute for the Compilation and Publication of the Works of Imam Khomeini, International Affairs Division, Tehran, 1995.

Khafajee, A., *Maqatil al-Ma'sumeen*, Ya'siz Zahra, Qom, 2008.

al-Khawarizmi, M., *Maqtal al-Hussain*, Dar al-Kitab al-Islami, 1979.

Kho'i, A., *Mu'jam al-Rijaal al-Hadith*, Manshuraat Madinat ul-Ilm, Qom, 1983.

Kho'i, A., *The Prolegomena to the Qur'an*, Ansariyan Publications, Qom, 2000.

Kilbani, A., *Hal Tazwuj Umar bi Umm Kulthum?*, Dar al-Mahajatu al-Baydha', Dar al-Esmah, Lebanon, 2007. Available at www.daralmahaja.com [Accessed on 27 October 2011]

Kulayni, Y., *al-Kafi*, Khurasan Islamic Research Centre, 1978.

Luqmani, *Eternal Manifestations*, Published as an E-book by Ahlul Bayt DILP 2006. http://www.al-islam.org/eternalmanifestations [Accessed on 27 October 2011]

al-Majlsi, M.B., *Hayat al-Qulub*, First Edition, Ansariyan Publications, Qom, 2003.

al-Majlisi, M.B., *Mir'at al-Uqool*, Dar al-Kutub al-Islamiya, Tehran, 1404 AH.

al-Mas'udi, A., *Muruj ad-Dhahab*, 1966, Universite Libanaise, Beirut, 1966.

Mavani, H., *Forward to Abu Mikhnaf's Maqtal*. Available in English at http://www.sicm.org.uk/knowledge/Kitab%20Maqtal%20al-Husayn.pdf [Accessed on 27 October 2011]

Milani, A., *Khabr Tazweej Umm Kulthum min Umar*, Shabkat al-Imamayn al-Hassanayn liltiraath wal fikr Islami. Available in Arabic at www.alhassanain.com [Accessed on 27 October 2011]

al-Mufid, *Kitab al-Irshad*, Ansariyan Publications, Qom, 2004, Third Edition.

al-Muhajir, A., *I'ilamu annee Fatima*, Dar al-Kitab wal Itrah, Beirut, 1993. Available in Arabic at http://al-muhajir.com/english/?page_id=883 [Accessed on 27 October 2011]

Munfared, A., *Imam Hussain and the Tragic Saga of Kerbala*, Ansariyan Publications, Qom, 2001, First Edition.

al-Muqarram, A., *Maqtal al-Husain*, Al-Kharsan Foundation for Publications, Beirut 2005. Available in English at www.al-islam.org/maqtal/ [Accessed on 27 October 2011]

Mutlaq, R. H., *The Last Luminary, I*slamic Publishing House, Canada, 2008.

Najafabadi, S., *Religious Extremism*, Organization for the Advancement of Islamic knowledge and Humanitarian Services, Montreal, Quebec, 2009.

Nisapuri, H., *al-Mustadrak al-Sahihain*, Hyderabad, 1915.

Ordoni, A., *Fatima the Gracious*, Ansariyan Publications, Qom, 1992.

Qarashi, B., *The Life of Fatima az-Zahra*, Ansariyan Publications, Qom, 2006, First Edition.

Qarashi, B., *The Life of Imam al-Hasan*, Ansariyan Publications, Qom, 2006, First Edition.

Qarashi, B., *The Life of Imam al-Hussain*, Ansariyan Publications, Qom, 2007, First Edition.

Qarashi, B., *The Life of Imam Zain al-Abideen*, Ansariyan Publications, Qom, 2000.

al-Qummi, A., *House of Sorrows*, Islamic Publishing House, Canada, 2010.

al-Qummi, A., *Nafas al-Mahmoom*, Islamic Study Circle, India, 2001. Available in English at http://www.al-islam.org/nafasulmahmum/) [Accessed on 27 October 2011]

al-Qummi, A., *Selections from Mafatih al-Jinan*, Ansariyan Publications, Qom, 2005.

Qummi, A., *Hayaat Amir al-Mo'mineen*, Intisharaat Kawthar Wilayat, Iran, 1419 AH.

Ibn Qutayba, *Al-Imamah wa Siyasah*, Matbaat al-Futuh al-Adabiya, Egypt, 1925.

Sadooq, *Al-Amaali*, The World Federation, 1998.

Sadooq, *Man La Yahdhuhul Faqih*, Dar at-Ta'arut, Beirut, 1981.

as-Sayuti, J., *The History of the Khalifahs who took the Right Way*, Ta-Ha Publishers Ltd, London, 2006.

Ibn Shadhan, *One Hundred Virtues of Ali ibn Abi Talib and His Sons, the Imams*, Ansariyan Publications, Qom, 2006.

Shahin, B., *Lady Zainab*, Ansariyan Publications, Qom, 2002.

Shahristani, A., *The Prohibition of Recording the Hadith*, Ansariyan Publications, Qom, 2004.

Shahristani, A., *Zawwaj Umm Kulthum*, Markaz al-Abhaath al-Aqaidiya, Qom, 2007. Availble in Arabic at www.alhassanain.com [Accessed on 27 October 2011]

Shahroodi, A., *Mustadrakaat 'Ilm al-Rijaal al-Hadith*, Shafaq Publishing, Tehran, 1412 AH.

Shakiri, H., *al-Mustapha wal Itrah*, Al-Hadi Nashr, Qom, 1415 AH.

Shirazi, H., *Mawsu'atu Kamila (Kalimat Syeda Zainab)*, Dar al-Ulum, Beirut, 2006.

Shirazi, H., Translated by S.M. Baqri, Z.,   *al-Hadith al-Qudsi*, Ansariyan Publications, Qom, 1999.

Suhani, J., *The Message*, Ansariyan Publications, Qom, 2004, Third Edition.

Tabatabai, M.H., *al-Mizan*, World Organisation for Islamic Services, Tehran, 2002.

Tabari, M., *Tareekh at-Tabari*, Mua'ssasatu al-A'lami lil Matbu'at, Beirut 1998 and 2007, State University of New York Press

Takim, L., *The Heirs of the Prophet*, State University of New York Press, New York, 2006.

al-Yaf'i, A., *Mir'at al-Jinan*, Mu'assasat ar-Risalat, Beirut, 1984.

Ya'qubi, A., *Tareekh Ya'qubi*, Mu'assasah al-A'lami lil Matu'at, Beirut, 1977.

Zubaydee, M., *500 Questions Regarding the Women around Syeda Zahra*, Dar al-Hujjatu al-Baydha', Beirut, 2007.

Zumaizam, S., *Nisaa al-Hawla al-Hussain*, Dar al-Jawadain, Lebanon, 2011.

Appendix 1

Transliteration Chart

In the sections where Arabic words and phrases have been commentated on, diacritic marks have been added to show the exact pronouncation of the word. The following chart is a guide to the transliteration system adopted in this book which is also used by the *International Journal of Middle Eastern Studies*.

ء	'	ز	z	ق	q	Long vowels	
ب	b	س	s	ك	k	ا	ā
ت	t	ش	sh	ل	l	و	ū
ث	th	ص	ṣ	م	m	ي	ī
ج	j	ض	ḍ	ن	n	Short vowels	
ح	ḥ	ط	ṭ	ه	h	´	a
خ	kh	ظ	ẓ	و	w	´	u
د	d	ع	ʿ	ي	y	ِ	i
ذ	dh	غ	gh	ة	ah		
ر	r	ف	f	ال	al		

Appendix 2

The Salutation on Lady Umm Kulthum

This salutation is from *A Complete Manual of Short Ziyarat and Salutations*, Published by the Al-Mahdi Institute

السَّلامُ عَلَيْكِ يا بِنْتَ سَيِّدِ الأنبيآء

Peace be upon you, the daughter
of the Master of the Prophets

السَّلامُ عَلَيْكِ يا بِنْتَ صَاحِبِ الْحَوْضِ وَاللِوَاءِ

Peace be upon you, the daughter
of the Owner of the Pool and the Brigade

السَّلامُ عَلَيْكِ يا بِنْتَ صَاحِبِ الْمَقَامِ الْمَحْمُوْدِ

Peace be upon you, the daughter
of the Owner of the Praised Position

السَّلامُ عَلَيْكِ يا بِنْتَ خَيْرِ خَلْقِ اللهِ

Peace be upon you, the daughter
of the Best of God's creation

السَّلامُ عَلَيْكِ يا بِنْتَ يَعْسُوْبِ الدِّيْنِ

Peace be upon, you the daughter
of the Protector of the Religion

السَّلامُ عَلَيْكِ يا بِنْتَ أَمِيْرِالْمُؤْمِنِيْنَ

Peace be upon you, the daughter
of the Commander of the Faithful

السَّلامُ عَلَيْكِ يا بِنْتَ خَلِيْفَةِ سَيِّدِ الْمُرْسَلِيْنَ

Peace be upon you, the daughter
of the Caliph of the Master of the Messengers

السَّلامُ عَلَيْكِ يا بِنْتَ فاطِمَةَ الزَّهْراءِ

Peace be upon you, the daughter of Fatima Al-Zahra

السَّلامُ عَلَيْكِ يا بِنْتَ يَا اُمَّ الْمَصائِب

Peace be upon you, the daughter of the Mother of Tragedies

يَا اُخْتَ الْحُسَيْنِ الشَهِّيْدِ يَا اُمَّ كُلْثُوْم

O the sister of Hussain the Martyr, O Umm Kulthum

وَرَحْمَةُ اللهِ وَبَرَكاتُهُ

And God's mercy and blessings be upon you

Appendix 3

Poetry about
Lady Umm Kulthum

A Poem Honouring Her Status
By Abbas and Shabbir Tejani (written for this book)

*The lady of light, the highest of high, the teacher of life,
Umm Kulthum*

Your history and your life has been blurred
But we will make sure that it's uncovered
We promise that you will be remembered
The way you should be, oh hidden treasure
This has become our living aim
On our hearts is engraved your name
Your love will shine brightly like a flame

*The lady of light, the highest of high, the teacher of life,
Umm Kulthum*

You are the granddaughter of Mustafa
The daughter of Zahra and Murtadha

The sister of Hassan al Mujtaba
And of Hussain Sayyed-ash-Shuhada
Their holy blood courses through your veins
Within you their purity remains
Who else on this earth can hold this claim?

The lady of light, the highest of high, the teacher of life,
Umm Kulthum

Oh holy lady this is your station
You gave your life to save this religion
This was your love and your dedication
For all of us you're an inspiration
The angels are sending you salaam
Because you saved the faith of Islam
By sacrificing without a qualm

The lady of light, the highest of high, the teacher of life,
Umm Kulthum

Your name came from the highest of ladies
Because of the likeness of your qualities
She also stood up against the enemies
She was the noble sister of Moses
She helped her brother to preach the faith
By practicing and preaching with grace
Like her, your name will not be erased

The lady of light, the highest of high, the teacher of life,
Umm Kulthum

Your father Haider was never subdued
He stood by you and so dearly loved you
He guarded you like a father would do

In every matter, for every issue
For all of those who think otherwise
Do you not think that Ali would rise?
Or are you suggesting he compromised?

The lady of light, the highest of high, the teacher of life,
Umm Kulthum

Those cowardly hypocrites were gloating
The haters of Ali were celebrating
How must their actions have left you feeling?
You spoke with vigour and left them reeling
You are the fearless without a doubt
The eloquence in which you spoke out
Encapsulated your love throughout

The lady of light, the highest of high, the teacher of life,
Umm Kulthum

The scholars all unanimously write
Your father stayed on his very last night
Of life at your house, Oh Lady of Light
Such was your status that this was your right
This fact has gone down in history
That he revered you undoubtedly
This is a sign of your purity

The lady of light, the highest of high, the teacher of life,
Umm Kulthum

The proclamation you made in Kufa
That we're not permitted any sadaqah
Because we are the daughters of Zahra

And are the granddaughters of Mustafa
By saying this fact you opened eyes
And people started to recognise
What is the truth and what are the lies

The lady of light, the highest of high, the teacher of life,
Umm Kulthum

From Kerbala to the tyrant's palace
You told the world of your holy status
You told them of your grandfather's greatness
And how you were all paraded veil-less
This message people could not ignore
In Kufa and Shaam there was uproar
You shook that empire to its core

The lady of light, the highest of high, the teacher of life,
Umm Kulthum

Do not accept us or give us greetings
These verses you said before entering
The city where you were born and living
These words forever will be resonating
Today the *zakirs* repeat your words
They are recited throughout the world
In *marsiyahs* and from the minbar

The lady of light, the highest of high, the teacher of life,
Umm Kulthum

We ask Allah through your intercession
To let us show each other compassion
And rid this whole world of all oppression

Enabling us to achieve progression
Teach us to live our lives in your way
To follow your footsteps everyday
So that from Allah we never stray

The lady of light, the highest of high, the teacher of life,
Umm Kulthum

AN ELEGY FOR LADY UMM KULTHUM
By Abbas and Shabbir Tejani (2008/2009 volume, track 4)[1]

A shower of stones rains upon the ladyfolk of the Ahlul Bayt
And there is not even a cloth on the head of Umm Kulthum

Qasim and Akbar are no longer present
Even little Ali Asghar is not present
"There is no one to aid us"
On the lips of Umm Kulthum is this lament

Zainab brought (to Kerbala) Aun and Muhammad
And sacrificed them (in the path of Allah)
The pain in the heart of Umm Kulthum was
"Who can I sacrifice for Imam Hussain?"

Abbas came into the tents and saw
Umm Kulthum was sitting with
her head bowed and crying
(So he said) *"Oh sister, in your name*
I will go and sacrifice myself"

How can Umm Kulthum forget that scene
The tents were burning and the veils were being snatched

---

1 Translated from Urdu

From the burning tents, Zainab brought Abid
Upon her back, becoming the Abbas of the caravan

When Sham-e-Ghariba ("The night of the Orphans")
came
Little Sakinah wandered into the battlefield
Umm Kulthum wandered after her
All alone and without an aide

Little Sakinah stood in Damascus
On the spears the head of her father
People are jeering from every corner
Who can protect now, the Imam's daughter

The head of Abbas, the veil's protector
Isn't staying on top of the spear
When Umm Kulthum entered the courtyard
Her brother Abbas couldn't stand to see her

How can the daughter of Ali walk
All around her are drunkards
The tyrants surround the family of Imam Hussain
How can the family of the Prophet proceed?

In the courtyard when the tyrant asked
"Who from you is Zainab?"
The door of the courtyard cried out
"Where are you, oh victor of Khaybar?"

This our wish, oh Umm Kulthum
When "Tejani brothers" recite
At every moment, keep upon our heads
The shadow and protection of the flag of Abbas

The Suffering of Lady Umm Kulthum
By Syed Irfan Haider, 2005 volume, track 2

[1]

When the Syed women came into the markets of Shaam, they bought the sand from the deserts on their hair rather than their veil. Poor Kulthum's gaze fell on Abbas, by that time Abbas had thrown his head from the spear, on to the desert sands.

Chorus: There is a scared look on Kulthum's face that her gaze shouldn't fall upon him, Abbas' head won't stay up on the spear.

What more pain can this loyal servant face then to see those ladies hair when he had protected their veil, oh people of Shaam where is your guilt?
Abbas' head won't stay up on the spear

When Sakinah fell to the ground in utter disbelief, her aunty said "look at this bond between uncle and niece oh my *khuda*, this poor little girl lies broken hearted in the sand". *Abbas' head won't stay up on the spear.*

The people of Shaam made a spectacle of themselves along with the Syed ladies, homeless and with their open hair, where do they find any support? All of Allah's creations cry tears of blood for them.
Abbas' head won't stay up on the spear.

"Throw the sand in the air to create a veil for them", was the cry of Zainab that was heard throughout the land, the sky and the ground cried and said:

---

1 Translated from Urdu

Abbas' head won't stay up on the spear.
Sajjad cried tears of blood when he saw innocent little
Sakinah slapped repeatedly by the cursed man, his head-
less body moved around in pain by the river bank.
Abbas' head won't stay up on the spear.

Oh those of you who grieve for them, Ali's daughter was
open haired in the markets of Shaam, When his head fell
to the ground the people where surprised, the evil man
asked Abid tell us why won't
Abbas' head won't stay up on the spear.

Throughout their whole journey the Queen of the Universe was with them all the way, The Nabi recites a *noha*
while sand is thrown in the air by Hassan and Ali, what a
time this is when Sarwar cries on his chest.
Abbas' head won't stay up on the spear.

Sometimes it's Layla sometimes it Farwa, sometimes it's
Kulthum who weeps uncontrollably, Hiding her face with
her hair Zainab cried and said: *"Mother look at these scenes
of sadness and pain"*.
Abbas' head won't stay up on the spear.

While writing this noha, Irfan and Mazhar cried and said
there is no worse tragedy that could have befallen the
children of the Prophet, we cried our hearts and souls out
after writing only one line.
Abbas' head won't stay up on the spear.

LADIES OF THE AHLUL BAYT
By Syed Nadeem Sarwar, 2002 volume, track 4[1]

Chorus:
When Kulthum lifted the curtain of the house
When Kulthum lifted the curtain of the house
It was our land once
I saw the loved one

The granddaughter of the Nabi opened her heart and
cried
There was silence everywhere in Allah's land
(The ones who had left Bani Hashim)
She saw her old neighbourhood

Those streets where Aun and Mohammed used to play
That's where Abdullah walked, quiet and alone
(In every direction)
I saw an ocean of children
I saw the loved one

Sughra heard the news the traveller had come back
She was happy that someone was at the Nabi's *roza*
(What did Sughra think?)
What did she see?

The hair was open and their arms empty
Only shadows of Asgher and Sakinah's earrings
(Abbas' *alam*)
Was the only one to be seen

When they stopped at their grandfather's *roza*

---

1 Translated from Urdu

She fell in pain on the dusty ground
(Her grandfather's crying face)
Was seen by her

Sughra asked her mum: "Why are your arms empty?"
The pain went through her but she said nothing
(She started crying when)
She saw the burning crib

She entered the house without her brother
She was filled with emotion but her soul was strong
(When she saw)
The tattered body of her brother without the *kafan*

Qasim and Akbar are nowhere to seen
She said I had left this big house
(I searched for them)
In and around every grave

Aun and Mohammed's beds were made there
And all of Asgher's toys were all there
(But nobody was there to play)
That I could see

Poetry From Three Famous Iraqi Poets

By Sheikh Abdul Wahhab al-Kaashi¹, reciting as if he was Lady Umm Kulthum²:

And the fear invites itself, and yet there is no protector
from it.

---

1 See al-Kaashi, *at-Tareeq ila Mambr al-Hussain*, vol. 8, page 365
2 Translated from Arabic

And the heart is beating, and I bring forth tears

Oh the crier of the hardships of the bare land!
Remain with a deep secret and do not become weary, be a
propagator

Tell, from my tongue, the Prophet
Give the news from him and everything will tremble

Oh grandfather! The whips of the enemies is so painful it
causes me to die and their curse to Haider is worse still
Oh our grandfather, they have torched our tents, the fire
surrounded our place

Oh our grandfather, there is no eye that cried for us
Except the whips answered back to us and we were cursed
by them

The suckling baby dried from the thirst
And their pouring of water to him was their arrows

Oh Grandfather! Water was made forbidden for my
brother and his blood was made lawful
Oh Grandfather! We left your beloved bare and his chest
was torn into parts

Oh Grandfather! The sun changed our faces and the
enemies did not have mercy
Can you be patient while the birds have eaten their flesh?

By Sha'bi[1], reciting as if he was Imam al-Hussain speaking to Lady Umm Kulthum[2]:

Oh my sister, what has caused you to cry, while we are
the pillars
Except for Sajjad as, for me, he is all alone

Even my baby son, his throat was cut off, it has become a
calamity for him
For tomorrow it becomes the arrows

And my chest, oh my sister, is the battleground for horses
after my murder
You will cry for me, going here and there

And my body will be left bare for three days on the sand
And my body will become absorbed by the sand

And in my deepest, oh my sister, while the fires are
burning the tents
I will wish to come and protect the women

At that time the people have no mercy, I fear that no one
among them will come to aid you
And after this follows the pains of the orphans

From the arrogance of the captors, by the arrogance of
Damascus
The Great and Beautiful, oh the daughter of the best of
creation, seeing the committed and firm

---

1 See al-Kaashi, *at-Tareeq ila Mambr al-Hussain*, vol. 8, page 366
2 Translated from Arabic

My sister, he shouted the barking of a dog and the noise
will vanish!
So ask from the calamity and the atrocities of my
patience!

Ask me to see you while the blood from my beard is
dripping
Ask my patience from my trial and tribulation

By Abu Dhiyyah[1], reciting as if he was Lady Umm Kulthum[2]:

Oh the one who has committed a crime against Allah!
Oh criminal, you don't listen and you intend toward the
same!
Does he remain bare on the sand for the sake of making
happy the evil ruler?

---

1 See *at-Tareeq ila Mambr al-Hussain*, vol. 8, page 366
2 Translated from Arabic